Self-Discipline

Mental Toughness Mindset:
Increase Your Grit and Focus to Become a Highly Productive (and Peaceful!) Person

Positive Psychology Coaching Series

Copyright © 2017 by Ian Tuhovsky

Author's blog: www.mindfulnessforsuccess.com
Author's Amazon profile: amazon.com/author/iantuhovsky
Instagram profile: https://instagram.com/mindfulnessforsuccess

Important
The book is not intended to provide medical advice or to take the place of medical advice and treatment from your personal physician. Readers are advised to consult their own doctors or other qualified health professionals regarding the treatment of medical conditions. The author shall not be held liable or responsible for any misunderstanding or misuse of the information contained in this book. The information is not indeed to diagnose, treat or cure any disease.
It's important to remember that the author of this book is not a doctor/therapist/medical professional. Only opinions based upon his own personal experiences or research are cited. The author does not offer medical advice or prescribe any treatments. For any health or medical issues – you should be talking to your doctor first.

Please be aware that every e-book and "short read" I publish is written truly by me, with thoroughly researched content 100% of the time. Unfortunately, there's a huge number of low quality, cheaply outsourced spam titles on the Kindle non-fiction market these days, created by various internet marketing companies. **I don't tolerate these books. I want to provide you with high quality, so if you think that one of my books/short reads can be improved in any way, please contact me at:**

contact@mindfulnessforsuccess.com

<u>I will be very happy to hear from you, because that's who I write my books for!</u>

Introduction

Each Day In Life is Training
Training For Myself
Though Failure is Possible
Living Each Moment
Equal to Anything
Ready for Everything
I am Alive - I am This Moment
My Future Is Here and Now
For if I cannot Endure Today
When and Where Will I.

-(Words for Each Day) Soen Ozeki Daisen-in Zen Temple, Kyoto

Some people just seem to have it all. They're the ones with the great jobs, the perfect bodies, and gorgeous spouses. They even have the energy to get up in the morning and go to the gym! Their self-belief is unshakeable. When they want to get something done, they damn well go and do it. To most of us, they appear god-like.

OK, so I exaggerated slightly. No-one has a completely perfect life. On the other hand, some of us get pretty close. What separates these lucky folks from the majority? What is it about them that draws in success after success, opportunity after opportunity? You'll have noticed that these amazing people also have the remarkable ability to remain optimistic and stoic even when everything around them begins to unravel.

Going further, have you ever wondered how those working and living in extreme conditions manage to keep on going without giving up? Some of them even seem to enjoy the challenge! You've probably heard about Special Ops squads who spend weeks on near-impossible missions, or explorers who trek through bitterly cold climates for months on end. Other exceptional individuals lead lives of another sort of intense focus and concentration. The average day in the life of a Buddhist monk in the Zen tradition, for example, consists primarily of prayer and meditation. They forsake the temptations of the material world and focus on spiritual development at the highest level. They are the religious equivalents of Olympic gymnasts and the most successful CEOs. How do they stay so motivated? What drives them? **The answer to all these questions boils down to a single word – self-discipline.** You see, it isn't really about luck at all. Sure, some people are born with the genes that make them better-looking or happier than the average individual. But what really elevates a regular Joe or Jane to superhero status is laser-sharp focus, perseverance, and the ability to keep on going when everyone else would have quit. **In this book, you are going to learn their secrets.**

If you've ever wondered why you never quite live up to your potential, then this is the guide you've been waiting for. If you are sitting on a pile of hopes and dreams that never go anywhere, get ready to change your life! You are about to learn the secret that underpins every top athlete, CEO, and performer. You are going to discover exactly how some of the world's toughest individuals, including Navy SEALs, routinely stare danger in the face and come out on top.

Some of what you read may shock you. For instance, did you know that motivation is actually a very poor foundation on which to rely if you want to achieve true greatness? It's true! Even those who can honestly say they love their jobs or have found their true purpose in life don't always wake up in the morning raring to go. **It isn't the most motivated who win in this life, it's the most self-disciplined.** For reasons you will discover later in the book, motivation is best thought of as a nice side dish rather than the main entrée when it comes to self-discipline.

Neither is it necessary to be happy in order to be successful. In fact, you may be surprised to learn what happiness really means, and why most of us go looking for it in all the wrong places. If you think that you will become happy through achieving everything you want with minimal effort, you are going to severely limit what you get in life. It's time to break away from everything you thought you knew about contentment, fulfilment and motivation. Once you understand what really drives us as human beings – here's a hint, it's not actually money – and fulfils our deepest needs, you can hack your mindset and attain military-level self-discipline.

Why does this topic matter so much to me? I didn't appreciate the importance of self-discipline until my early thirties. I'd worked for several well-known corporations, excelling at most of my roles in their HR departments. Yet something was always missing. I felt like I was losing control over my own career. After all, however senior my position, ultimately my job role and paycheck were always determined by someone else.

My typical pattern would go like this: I'd apply for an exciting new job, spend the first year or so getting to know the company culture, but then feel a creeping sense of claustrophobia at about the 18-month mark. I'd start to get a little itchy. I'd daydream about quitting my corporate career and becoming self-employed. What would it be like to work for myself? Yet whenever I tried to imagine actually setting up my own business and taking complete responsibility for my life, I hit a wall. As much as I wanted to make a new start, I couldn't quite make the leap. How would I motivate myself to continually seek out new clients? Who would hold me accountable for my schedule? It all seemed so daunting. As you can imagine, I felt pretty anxious. I was at a crossroads.

What finally changed everything for me? A single conversation. One morning I was sitting in the coffee room with a much older colleague. I'll call him "Mark." Mark had been in his role for nearly ten years, and it was no secret that he hated his job. We were making idle chit-chat about the vacations we'd most like to take that year, and I confessed that for some time I'd wanted to set up my own business and travel the world, moving from country to country whilst working as a consultant.

He laughed. "Yeah right," he said. "No-one ever does that." As he walked back to his desk, a wave of nausea washed over me. *So this is what defeat feels like,* I thought. *He's right. I couldn't do that. It's a dream. I don't have it in me – or do I?*

At that point, I had a choice to make. I could either have stayed where I was, talking about the same problems and unfulfilled ambitions year after year, or I could make a radical change. I had a few self-help books lying around, some of them unopened gifts. There and then I decided to dive into the world of positive psychology and self-development and learn how to achieve whatever I wanted.

As it turned out, I was asking the wrong questions all along! I had been held back by the belief that I had to feel completely sure of myself and permanently motivated before I could become successful. I was also under the impression that once I was "a success," my life would magically sort itself out and I'd be happy. I had so much to learn.

Countless hours of reading, reflection, and experimentation later, I not only run my own HR consultancy business but have also set down all my favorite findings and top tips for self-discipline in this book. I don't want anyone else to be held back by a lack of self-belief. If you really want to grow your self-discipline and transform your life, you can. I now lead a life greater than any I could have imagined a decade ago and yes, I consider myself highly self-disciplined. I'm by no means perfect – I'll share a few of my own mistakes as we go through this book – but the younger me would be pleasantly surprised at how far I've come. **If I can do it, so can you.** This book is presented in two parts. The first part will tell you everything you need to know to shift your mindset from self-doubt and ambivalence to pure self-discipline. You'll learn what psychology, philosophy, and even the military can tell us about motivation and what drives us to change.

The second part goes further and focuses on practical strategies you can start using today to supercharge every area of your life. You'll discover how routines, goal-setting and a little-known approach called Morita Therapy will allow you to push yourself harder than ever before.

Self-discipline isn't taught as skill in schools. Once you've read this book you may feel tempted to launch a campaign to make it a mandatory part of the curriculum, but we aren't quite there yet. This means it's on us as adults to learn how to take back our willpower and give ourselves the edge. Fortunately, we live in an age of information and can easily research any number of psychological theories and techniques that will help us excel. Self-development has become something of an addiction for me over the past few years, and once you've read this book you'll understand why! So many people, from psychologists to monks, have much to teach us about self-discipline. It is an honor to pass this priceless information onto you.

Ian Tuhovsky

Your Free Mindfulness E-book

I really appreciate the fact that you took an interest in my work!

I also think it's great you are into self-development and proactively making your life better.

This is why I would love to offer you a free, complimentary 120-page e-book.

It's about Mindfulness-Based Stress and Anxiety Management Techniques.

It will provide you with a solid foundation to kick-start your self-development success and help you become much more relaxed, but at the same time, more focused and effective person. All explained in plain English, and it's a useful free supplement to this book.

To download your e-book, please visit:

http://www.tinyurl.com/mindfulnessgift

Enjoy!
Thanks again for being my reader! It means a lot to me!

Chapter 2: Success Is A Process, Not A Moment Of Glory

If you are serious in your pursuit of success, you need to have a realistic grasp of what it really entails. For most people, the term "success" conjures up an image of a winner celebrating their hard-earned achievement. You may think of the athlete collecting a medal before standing on the podium, the CEO selling their company in a billion-dollar transaction, or a dieter finally hitting their goal weight.

What do all these imagined scenarios have in common? They are all based on the assumption that to be a success is to work towards a single goal that can be objectively judged by outsiders. Maybe it isn't surprising that we think this way, given how our school system operates. Everything is boiled down to grades and numbers, with focus placed more on a single letter or score than the means by which we actually get there.

In fact, success is not a single achievement, or even a series of achievements. It is an ongoing process. Successful people know that **victory is a state of mind** and actively **cultivate it on a daily basis**. Have you ever heard the saying, "It takes a long time to become an overnight success?" It's a cliché because it's absolutely true. No-one wakes up one morning having miraculously attained all they desired with no effort. This just isn't how the real world works. If you are guilty of magical or wishful thinking, you need to drop the habit fast if you are to master self-discipline and achieve anything of note. You are not exempt from the rules of the universe. If you want something, you are going to have to learn patience and find enjoyment in hard (and smart!) work.

Don't forget too that goals, once met, often require maintenance. If your definition of "success" only describes the moment you hit a goal, you'll neglect to keep up your results. The classic example is that of someone trying to lose weight. Most of us will relate to this scenario. How many times have you tried to lose a few pounds, only to start regaining the weight at twice the speed you lost it? I for one have been through a similar cycle several times, except that in my case I was trying to increase my muscle mass. I would make promising gains but then after a couple of months lose them. This was a frustrating process. Immense self-discipline is needed to keep up the healthy eating and exercise that bought you the weight loss in the first place. The fact that most dieters regain the weight they have lost is testament to this fact. If you approach the task of weight loss with only the final number in mind, you are setting yourself up for long-term failure.

The Japanese have long since recognized the importance of framing success as a process and not an event. The philosophy of Kaizen, which translates as "improvement" or "good change" in English, refers to the practice of building on success via continuous small changes. Kaizen is mainly used in business settings, but it is also a useful tool for anyone interested in self-development. According to the Kaizen Institute UK, the key principles of this philosophy are that "good processes bring good results" and success is likely when you "take action to contain and correct root causes of problems."[1]

Kaizen therefore also asks us to take a good long look at how we are trying to achieve our goals in the first place. Most people decide that they want to manifest a particular outcome, yet give relatively little thought as to how they are going to go about making it happen or how they might make adjustments along the way. For example, you might decide to set a goal of "losing twenty pounds using a high-fat, low-carb diet over a three-month period." But what happens if you have lost very little weight four weeks into your diet, and aren't enjoying most of the foods you are

---

[1] Kaizen Institute UK. (2017). *What is Kaizen?* [uk.kaizen.com]

eating?

At this point, most dieters would quit, maybe wait a while and then try to motivate themselves to try again. However, if they decided to apply the Kaizen philosophy, their next step would be to look at what had been working well and what could be adjusted to improve their chances of losing weight. For example, their exercise regimen might be helping them feel healthier and more energetic and yet not result in significant weight change. Applying the principles of Kaizen, they could make small alterations that nevertheless make a big impact on the final outcome. For example, they may choose to persist with the same type of exercise but work out more often and for shorter periods of time.

Adopting a Kaizen approach also prevents you from falling into the trap of "when...then" thinking. When you view success as an event, you run the risk of forgetting that in order to reap the rewards, you have to first lay down the foundations. Have you ever heard someone else say something like, "When I get a great job, I'll be happy" on a regular basis yet never actually take steps to change their situation? This is "when...then" thinking at its finest. Kaizen challenges us to see success as a cycle of achievement, improvement, further achievement, further improvement, and so on. It assumes that we have never completely fulfilled our potential. There is no end point. Things could always be better, and we need to be proactive in identifying the route that will get us there in an efficient manner.

In my case, I wanted to set up my own business. The trouble was, I was too busy thinking about the day everything would finally fall into place and daydreaming about being able to hand in my notice. Often I would totally forget that I'd need to take numerous small steps along the way! Whenever I reminded myself that I'd need to sit down at some point and come up with a business plan, a budget, and a marketing strategy my brain would shut down. I told myself that I'd get round to it "someday," and then I'd be ready to enter the next phase of my life. For years, that day never came. If I hadn't bothered to learn more about self-discipline, I'd probably still be stuck in an office making a decent living but not really enjoying my life.

When I finally did sit down and sketch out a business plan, it quickly became apparent that I would need to undertake further research. I spent a few weeks looking into my target market, reviewing the online platforms I could potentially use to reach out to new clients, and flipping through my contacts list to find people who could help launch my business via personal recommendations and word-of-mouth marketing. At that point, I had recently become familiar with the Kaizen philosophy and was willing to rework my plans several times as new information became available. Although it sounds like a lot of work – and it was! – it was also liberating. **I no longer expected to get everything right the first time around**, and so my anxiety about setting out on my own lessened.

Taking the first step and expecting it to yield less than perfect results also helps you avoid the most sinister aspect of "when...then" thinking. When you become too fixated on a particular outcome which may or may not manifest in the future (and if you are sitting around waiting for a flash of motivation, it's not going to manifest anytime soon), you miss out on the chance to enjoy life in the present. As practitioners of Zen will tell you, all we actually have is this present moment. The past has gone, with no hope of return. There is literally no way of changing what has already happened. The future has yet to arrive, and even if we can predict it with any degree of certainty, there is always the chance that we might be blindsided by unforeseen events. Whilst we can enjoy memories of the past and hope for the future, our lives can only be lived in the present.

This means that by daydreaming and half-heartedly planning what you want to happen instead of actively making your ambitions your reality, you are wasting precious time. When you appreciate just how much time it takes to attain and maintain any significant level of success, you won't be so willing to tolerate this mindset in either yourself or others. No-one knows how much time they have left on this planet, and frittering it away is incredibly wasteful.

So how can you actually start putting your most cherished plans into practice? You'd be forgiven for thinking that motivation is the key to sustaining the energy required to work towards success over a long period of time. However, as you are about to discover in the next chapter, motivation isn't as magical as you might believe.

Chapter 3: The Truth About Motivation

How many times have you heard someone say, "I just can't get motivated today," or "I'd love to do X, Y and Z, if only I had the motivation"? Maybe you've caught yourself saying something similar. Most of us have been raised to believe that if we just feel motivated to do something, it'll get done. **We live by the belief that if we sit around and wait long enough to feel some motivation or "drum up some willpower," everything will suddenly become so much easier.**

This is a great idea in theory. Motivation has probably worked for you at least occasionally. For example, you may have been motivated to spend hours searching for just the right gift for everyone on your Christmas list, because you want your friends and family to be happy. In this case, motivation would push you through those hours at the mall or tedious evenings comparing prices on various websites.

However, when it comes to the big stuff – losing weight, starting a business, writing a novel, and so on – motivation just isn't enough. Yes, you might feel a big rush of excitement at the beginning of your project, but over time your level of motivation will inevitably wax and wane. This is because once the reality of the situation kicks in, you start to realize that reaching your goal will entail some hard work. Your motivation will drop, and at this point you need to draw on other resources to power yourself through. This is why self-discipline and building positive habits are so important.

Stanford University psychologist Dr Kelly McGonigal is an expert in the science of willpower and self-discipline. In a 2014 interview for the TED Blog, she explains that when we are faced with a difficult task, two parts of our personality come into conflict.[2] One part of us is able to see into the future, and understands that pushing our own limits and being willing to tolerate some deprivation or psychological hardship will be well worth it in the end. However, there is also another part of us that seeks instant gratification, wants quick results, and is frustrated when we can't meet a goal with minimal effort. It is only when we can tap into that first part that we'll be able to overcome setbacks and achieve our goals. I also described this issue in more detail, along with the explanation on how to resolve internal conflicts between two opposing parts of our mind in my best-selling book, "Emotional Intelligence Training."

---

[2] May, K.T. (2014). *Kelly McGonigal on why it's so dang hard to stick to a resolution.* blog.ted.com

I found this very problem was one of my biggest blocks to leaving my 9-5 and establishing a new lifestyle as a self-employed consultant. Even though I had many good reasons for making the leap, the thought of sitting down and tackling the more mundane parts of my business life such as drawing up a marketing plan would make me groan. *I'll never be able to motivate myself to do that!* I'd think.

Fortunately, once I read up on how motivation really works I knew I'd never have to actually feel happy about the dull stuff. I just had to make sure that it got done, and not beat myself up when I felt less than elated at the thought of handling stacks of paperwork. Dr McGonigal notes that most people believe that they are lazy unless they feel consistently motivated, but in fact the struggle between our conflicting desires is simply part of what makes us human. Expect to feel apathetic sometimes, but don't use it as an excuse not to make progress.

To learn more about why motivation isn't sufficient when you need to get serious results, let's take a few lessons from people you might think need huge amounts of motivation – the special forces. Take the Navy SEALs, for example. These elite military officers must be ready and willing to undertake special operations under the sea, in the air or on land at any time. The Navy and the CIA work together to select only the best servicemen for these specialized operations, which are often extremely dangerous. Even to become a SEAL is an arduous task in itself, with only 20% of trainees even completing the first phase of their training.[3]

How many people are going to feel truly motivated to get up and undertake grueling tasks in hostile environments every day? Not many. One of their mottos is "The only easy day was yesterday." They never pretend that their job is easy, and they expect to face hardship on a regular basis. Yet the SEALs get things done – after all, they were the forces responsible for taking down Osama Bin Laden.

Yes, motivation in the traditional sense of simply wanting to get up and do something for the sake of it is one of the factors behind a SEAL's success. To be a SEAL is to command considerable respect from other military personnel, and affords an individual the opportunity to serve their country in a very direct and tangible way. Therefore, a SEAL's belief in these ideals will help them keep going in even the toughest of conditions. They are tapping into a **part of themselves that can see the big picture**, and remind themselves of why they have chosen to devote their careers to surviving various ordeals.

---

[3] NavySEALs.com. (2017). *BUD/S Prep: First Phase.* Navyseals.com

However, there is a second piece of the puzzle – **momentum**. In a talk given at the University of Texas 2014, Naval Admiral William H. McRaven passed on a valuable lesson he picked up during his time as a trainee SEAL. His instructors would insist on inspecting each trainee's bed to make sure it was made with military precision. The covers had to be squared neatly, the pillow positioned correctly, and the spare blanket placed perfectly in the barrack storage rack.

According to McRaven, the instructors were employing an effective piece of psychology. They believed that the act of making the bed was enough to trigger a sense of momentum in each trainee, and that this energy would carry them forward as they carried out their other tasks. The trainees didn't have to look deep within themselves to find enough motivation to last them throughout the day – they just had to commit to making their bed first thing in the morning, and the rest would follow.

You might have found that just getting the ball rolling is enough to power you through unpleasant tasks. It definitely works in my case. For example, when I get too caught up in my work, I sometimes put off doing my share of the chores. There is no way that I would ever willingly spend several hours doing the laundry, washing the floors, sorting out the fridge and all the other mundane tasks that need to be done if you want to avoid living in your own filth. My motivation when faced with a list of chores is pretty damn low.

However, if I just make a commitment to placing a few dishes in the dishwasher, it then seems like a small step to turn the dishwasher on. Those few dishes are my equivalent of a SEAL trainee making their bed. Whilst I'm near the kitchen worktop, I may as well reach over and wipe a surface...and so on. Within ten minutes I've usually worked up enough momentum to complete all the chores within an afternoon.

If you have always believed that you need to feel sufficiently motivated before attempting a task, then you might resist the idea that you can achieve almost anything you want without even particularly wanting to do it. **However, the conviction that motivation comes before action is limiting**, because pure and spontaneous motivation is rare. If you are still skeptical, experiment with the momentum idea above. **Just get started, and you will soon come to appreciate that action encourages action, which may give rise to motivation as a happy side-effect.**

In summary, motivation can be a real asset. **It's particularly powerful if you are committed to a cause or a set of ideals.** Just consider how many people have decided to dedicate their lives to charity work or enter a religious order! I'm certainly not saying that motivation should be dismissed altogether. However, it's best seen as a bonus that sometimes makes self-discipline a little easier. The smartest strategy is to anticipate that the part of your brain obsessed with instant gratification will put up a real fight when you commit to a long-term task. Luckily, with the right mindset and the tools you will learn in the second half of this book, it can be tamed.

Chapter 4: You Always Have A Choice

As human beings, there is plenty we cannot control. We can't choose our parents. We can't pick and choose our ideal genetic makeup. We can't make others treat us exactly how we would like. At the same time, you have more power than you realize to make choices that will make your life significantly easier. In this chapter, I'm going to tell you why life is best thought of as a never-ending series of choices. When you start thinking of life in terms of options and consequences, the decision-making process will suddenly seem much easier.

When you are confronted by a problem, you have a decision to make. It comes down to this: What are you going to do about it? **There is absolutely no get-out clause here.** You can't choose not to take part in life. Even if you throw your hands up in the air and say "I'll just let this problem take care of itself!" **you are still making a choice.** Specifically, you are choosing to let other people or any number of unpredictable variables make the decision for you.

I admit that I've taken the let's-just-see-how-it-works-out option a few times. Once I had to share an office with one of my HR assistants. I was assured that the situation would be only temporary whilst the office manager reorganized the department workspace. A week passed, and no-one could tell me when my new officemate was scheduled for departure. I had nothing against the woman, but she had an insatiable appetite for a) celebrity gossip and b) those strange fruity herbal teas you can buy in health food stores. By the end of the second week, the room smelled of hibiscus and I knew more about the Kardashians than I did about the company development plan.

I hadn't been in the job long, so I was reluctant to make myself any enemies. I decided that I'd ask to work from home when possible, and use the opportunity to hone my ability to concentrate even with distractions around me. As it turned out, she chose to leave the company just two weeks later. The best part was that because she was also new and still working her probationary period, she left straightaway.

Obviously in this case everything worked out for the best, but in general I wouldn't recommend taking such a passive approach. For the sake of your own sanity and autonomy, it's better to think in terms of which choice you are going to pursue.

In order to reach a goal, you have to actively choose one uncomfortable outcome over another. For example, suppose you have always wanted to write a novel. You have a decision to make –

are you going to choose the pain associated with actively pursuing this ambition, or are you going to suffer the pain of regret that comes with letting your creative dreams slide?

You can choose to forego some of your leisure time every week so that you can make steady progress on your novel. This will cause you suffering in the sense that you will have to cut down the time you spend on pleasurable activities. You may also have to justify your choice to nosy family and friends who will keep asking you how the book is coming along. (As an amateur novelist myself, I can testify that this will indeed happen.) However, you stand a far better chance of actually reaching your goal if you make a start and then stick with your writing schedule. It won't always be fun and there will be times when your motivation will fly out the window, but as you now know, you don't need motivation to get results.

Your other option is not to write your novel, and continue with your usual routine. This will ensure that you don't experience any of the discomforts above, and that you are protected from the risk of failure. On the other hand, you will still find yourself regretting the fact that you've never managed to sit down and crank out that story whirring around in your head.

The first time you think about life in this way, it can feel rather depressing. **Yet realizing that your life is made up of a series of choices between various kinds of problems is empowering.** It'll give you back a feeling of control and higher purpose to know that your choices are based on the inevitable consequences of your actions. This is what being a responsible adult is really about – appreciating that there are seldom any easy answers, and being disciplined enough to choose the path that will take you where you need to go regardless of the sacrifices demanded of you to get there.

We all know people who believe that their actions are fruitless, that the world is out to get them, and that their efforts are doomed to failure. These people tend to become depressed and anxious. When you think that everything that happens to you is determined by powers beyond your control, there doesn't seem to be much point even in living.

To use a term from psychology, it's all about your locus of control. Psychologist Julian Rotter devised this theory in the 1950s and 1960s[4] to explain why some people blamed or credited themselves for everything in their lives whereas others always looked for someone or something else for "the reason why."

---

[4] Rotter, J. (1966). Generalized expectancies for internal versus external control of reinforcement. *Psychological Monographs, 80, (1),* 1-28.

A "locus" is a place where something happens. Your locus of control refers to your perception of what controls the events that unfold in your life, and subsequently influences how you react. If you have an external locus of control, you see life as something that happens to you. Even if something wonderful happens, you will ascribe it to external forces beyond your sphere of influence. For example, someone with an external locus of control who does well on an exam will put their success down to easy exam questions or a generous marker rather than their own ability or time spent in preparation.

On the other hand, if you have an internal locus of control, you will assume that you have always played an active role in bringing about any and all outcomes. For example, you are likely to attribute exam success to your own intelligence and the hours you spent learning the material. When you work from an internal locus of control, self-discipline will become much easier. You believe that you not only have the power to make the right choices, but when they pay off you'll be rightly deserving of all the credit. Making a plan of action and then carrying it out will seem like a great use of your time because it's bound to give you the results you want. An internal locus of control without self-discipline will only lead to disaster, because you'll believe that you are responsible for your life yet lack the ability to actually implement any constructive plans. This isn't a good place to be as it promotes self-blame.

There is no reason why those with an external locus of control cannot lead perfectly decent lives. It's far too simplistic to say that an internal locus is better for everyone in all situations. You probably know someone who is happy to just "go with the flow" and is content to accept whatever happens. However, given that you've picked up this book, I'm willing to bet you aren't one of them! You'll be more successful and feel more fulfilled only when you couple an internal locus of control with good self-discipline.

So why is it that some of us are "internals" and others "externals"? It comes down to your experiences in early life. If you learned early on that you will be rewarded when you try to do the right thing, you are more likely to carry that lesson into adulthood. For example, if your parents and teachers rewarded you consistently when you succeeded in tidying your room or getting good grades, the young version of you will have worked out that success or failure is down to your own efforts. When you later had to choose a course of study or make your way in the world of work, you will naturally tend to put in plenty of effort to do the best you can.

If you don't already operate from an internal locus of control, it's up to you to change the way you think. You have a choice to make! Even if the adults in your childhood didn't teach you to make the link between your intentions and outcomes, there's no reason why you can't approach things differently now. In recent years we've learned that the human brain is more plastic than scientists previously imagined. Make it a habit to assume that whatever your current situation, it's up to you to weigh up the pros and cons of each possible choice and base your final decision on the consequences of each. This applies to every situation in life, from getting ahead at work to finding the right romantic relationship.

Chapter 5: Your Life's True Purpose

Imagine someone stopped you on the street and asked, "What's the whole point of your life, anyway?"

Once you'd gotten over the initial shock that someone would ask such an outrageous question, what would you say? If you are like most people, you might cobble together an answer that includes something about "being happy" or "leaving something behind for the next generation." If you are of a more cynical or scientific persuasion, you might say that there is absolutely no point of your existence and human life is just a natural by-product of evolution.

In this chapter, I'm going to explain how successful people give real meaning to their lives and find a never-ending sense of purpose in every single day. Note that this doesn't mean conjuring up a magical reserve of infinite motivation – you already know that this isn't the path to self-discipline or contentment. This is more about the bigger picture. The ultimate question. Just what *is* the point? The world can be a cruel place. In this age of non-stop news, it's hard to escape the fact that innocent people suffer every day. Inequalities of all kinds still persist. Everyone gets ill, and eventually everyone dies. It can be tempting to just roll over and give up!

Unless you have a strong faith in a particular religion or set of spiritual teachings, you've probably spent some time pondering why you exist and how you should make the most of your life. Most of us hit a phase during our teenage years in which we begin looking at the world around us with a new cynicism. The innocence of childhood wears off as we develop the intellectual ability to poke holes in the rules and norms of society.

Some of us find a higher purpose or cause to believe in. Others settle on a job or vocation that provides them with a sense of purpose. **Unfortunately, most of us learn to ignore that part of us that seeks to find the reason why anyone should bother getting up in the morning.** We fall into the routine of adulthood instead, focusing on just making it through another day. This works for a while, but there comes a time – usually in your thirties or forties – when that old question of meaning catches up with you again.

This is exactly what happened to me. I had a reasonably typical middle-class upbringing. There was no big trauma or abuse in my childhood. Nothing happened that made me think the world was an especially bleak or hopeless place. Then I turned 14, my parents divorced, and nothing seemed to make sense. Like plenty of other young people, I became depressed and even self-harmed on a few occasions. There didn't seem to be any point in carrying on. I looked at my parents with their boring jobs and failed relationships and thought adulthood didn't look too appealing.

Fortunately for me, I'd always been a good student and thanks to a couple of truly inspiring teachers I managed to leave school with decent grades. College life soon offered me lots of distractions from my existential angst. After all, it's hard to be too depressed when you're out partying every night of the week and chasing after girls. Once I graduated, I then had to pour all my efforts into searching for my first grown-up job. It wasn't until my late twenties that I started to give serious thought to why I was still alive. This ultimately triggered my interest in self-development and positive psychology. I wanted to know why some people seemed to find meaning even when things went wrong.

I discovered that there are two key ways in which you can give your life an endless sense of purpose, and they work together to set up a positive cycle. Both require you to take responsibility for your own life, i.e. to develop an internal locus of control. Once you are willing to step up and acknowledge that everything within your sphere of influence is your responsibility, you have laid the foundations for serious self-discipline.

The first path to finding purpose is by identifying and overcoming your internal weaknesses. Note that this does not mean that you have to beat yourself up or compare yourself to other people. Self-pity is not only unattractive, but it won't help you develop self-discipline. If you believe that you are a fundamentally flawed individual without hope of redemption, you aren't going to believe that the future holds any hope for you. You won't be willing to put in the work required to address those areas in which you could stand to improve. Instead, you first need to accept that you are human. Like all humans, you have a unique set of positive and negative traits. You have strengths, and you also have weaknesses. **There are no exceptions to the rule.** Even those at the very top of their fields are imperfect. **Your uniqueness means that there is no point in comparing yourself to others.** If you are competitive by nature this might be hard to accept, but doing so will change your life. Everyone is dealt a different set of genetics and life circumstances. Our purpose in life isn't to outdo everyone else. **It's to gain self-mastery, which is the most satisfying and enduring form of personal power.**

We not only need to tolerate our weaknesses, but actively embrace them! This might sound a bit crazy, but think about it. If we were all born perfect, life would be much less interesting. We'd never know the satisfaction that comes with self-improvement. We wouldn't get to experience the pleasure of being able to look back in time, compare our current selves to our past selves, and take healthy pride in how far we've come.

You cannot change how other people behave – at least, not on any meaningful level. If you are in a position of authority, you can force them into acting a certain way. To invest your precious time and energy into trying to shape other people is a complete waste. Instead, focus on yourself. This way, you'll find true fulfilment and feel significantly more powerful. The best news of all? You will always inhabit your own body, so your progress will be cumulative. When you make the mistake of trying to control others, all your efforts are rendered null and void the moment they move away, die, or simply choose to stop listening to you. Always make yourself your number one project.

If you like the idea of influencing those around you, the most effective way to go about it is still to fix yourself first. Why? Because people respect those who are willing to put in the work and suffer the pain required to better themselves. Sure, people will have to listen to you if you're "the boss" and they want to keep their jobs, or they happen to be your children and want to avoid being grounded on the weekend. **But you will only have a lasting influence when you demonstrate your willingness to recognize and tackle your own weaknesses first.** If you know that you are prone to depressive thinking or melancholy, get some therapy. If you tend to be disorganized, learn how to manage your time. For every internal weakness there is a solution – you just need the discipline to find and implement it.

The second sure-fire way to give your life meaning is by setting out to defeat external limitations. Take a moment to think about one of your idols. Chances are that they had to overcome numerous limitations in order to get where they are today. For example, take Oprah Winfrey. She's one of the richest and most influential women in the world. Millions have watched her show and cite her as an individual who has inspired them to live a different kind of life. Yet Oprah has faced numerous limitations. She spent her early childhood years in poverty, and was sexually abused on numerous occasions as a child and young adult. She gave birth to a baby at the age of fourteen. Tragically, her son died. Yet Oprah went on to become an outstanding high school student, gained a full scholarship to college, and then rapidly ascended the media ladder. Oprah's attitude to adversity has been key in propelling her to stardom. She firmly believes that any goal is attainable as long as you are willing to put in the work required, and that taking responsibility for your own success is vital.[5]

When you come up against an obstacle, don't take it personally. The world isn't out to get you – **it's just a fact of life that everyone has to overcome challenges on their way to meeting their biggest goals.** Every external limitation is an opportunity for you to flex your self-discipline and stay true to your vision. It's a chance to sharpen your problem-solving skills, take stock of the options in front of you and choose the best path based on the knowledge and skills you have available to you at the time. Remember, making choices is unavoidable.

If this all sounds like a lot of hard work, that's a great sign! It means that you appreciate that life is not easy and it never will be. Gaining true control over yourself and your destiny requires consistent self-discipline, but will also fill you with a strong and lasting sense of purpose.

---

[5] Economy, P. (2015). *19 Empowering Quotes From Oprah Winfrey.* Inc.com

Chapter 6: What You Really Want – & How To Get It

If you had to guess what it is that most people really want from life, what would you say? Lots of money, great health, immortality, good looks? If you believe the media, we are all continually striving for bigger bank balances, thinner bodies, and public adoration.

I'm going to propose another idea. **What if we assume that all everyone really wants is more control over their lives?** After all, you can have all the money and material possessions anyone could dream of, but if you feel as though your life is out of your own control you'll sink into a state of helplessness. Don't underestimate the power of autonomy and the deep satisfaction that comes with steering your own course through life.

When we feel as though we are losing control, **we don't just get annoyed – we panic.**

Death isn't the biggest fear we face as humans. If it was, there would hardly be any suicides. No-one would be brave enough to actually end their lives. What we cherish most (even if we don't consciously know about it) is being able to exercise our own judgment and make our own decisions. The sense of power over our own lives is what really matters to us on a psychological level. When this comes under threat, the emotional fallout can be devastating. **In other words, the loss of control is the biggest subconscious human fear.**

If you've ever had a panic attack, you'll know how terrifying it is to lose control over your own bodily functions. During a panic attack, a sufferer will often find themselves short of breath, experience waves of heat and ice sweeping through their body, and feel dizzy. Most worrying of all, panic attacks often entail a general feeling of "going crazy." Mental illness and psychosis are still widely feared in our society because they represent a loss of control over one's emotions, thoughts and even basic grip on reality.

When external events make us feel as though we stand no chance of getting our lives back on track, the results can be tragic. Most suicides and other tragedies come from the loss of control over one's life. For example, it is not uncommon for those who suddenly lose a lot of money or find themselves deep in debt to contemplate suicide. They may see no way out of their financial situation and desperately crave a permanent respite from the feeling of being trapped in a personal hell with no clear way out. Assisted suicides are usually chosen by people suffering from incurable pain. Their fear of death might be real, but it pales in comparison to the terror of living out their final days in agony, completely dependent on others.

Relationships are another common source of stress and feelings of helplessness. For example, the success of a romantic relationship depends on the willingness of two people to work together towards sustaining a partnership. When one decides to leave or pull away, this can trigger strong feelings of loss and grief. When you make a single person the center of your emotional universe, you are effectively giving them complete power over your emotional health. Yet people do this all the time, then wonder why they struggle to move on when their relationships end.

Regaining a sense of control over your life gives you the best chance of achieving whatever you want most. It also restores your dignity. No longer will you feel at the mercy of random events or the whims of other people. Sometimes you probably don't understand why you act the way you do, or what you ought to do next. Understanding and controlling yourself is hard enough. Why make life even more difficult by trying to control the behavior of others?

Successful people understand the importance of control. They aren't superhuman, they just understand that it builds momentum – once you feel in control of one area of your life, it soon tips over into others. **A commitment to taking back control of your life will soon create a "can-do" attitude.** Once you have this down, you can do anything!

Let me show you how this works in practice. I used to really hate the idea of working out. Sometimes I'd look at myself in the mirror and think that I could stand to gain some muscle so that I'd feel more confident about my body, but that's about as far as it would go. It certainly didn't make me actually commit to starting an exercise regimen. Sure, I knew that getting stronger and even ripped would have made me feel better about myself, but it wasn't enough to drive me to make changes.

Then my father suffered a stroke. He was home alone and fell down the stairs, where he lay for several minutes before my mother found him. Obviously he was much older than me and had never taken any interest in working out, but watching him grapple with a grueling physiotherapy regimen was a wake-up call. His therapist said that because he had been relatively weak before his stroke – the guy had never lifted weights or built up any real muscle mass - his recovery would be pretty slow. It was months before he could walk properly again. I vowed that I would never end up in a similar position. I wanted to be strong enough to bounce back if I had to, and to enjoy living in a state of good health for many years to come. Within a few weeks, I had signed up to a gym and made an appointment with a personal trainer. Now that I see working out as a way of safeguarding my health, it has become one of my top priorities.

When you set a new goal, make sure that whatever it is you wish to gain will increase the amount of control in your life. For example, starting your own business because you want to have more control over your career and where you live is an excellent motive, because this means that you are working towards a more autonomous life. To be more fulfilled you need to discard and eliminate everything that holds you back whilst working towards things that bring you joy.

I'd go so far as to argue that control and self-mastery are the keys to happiness. Turn to the next chapter to discover what really helps us feel content, and how to avoid typical pitfalls you might come across in your pursuit of happiness.

Chapter 7: The Surprising Truth About Happiness

What does it really mean to be happy, and is our modern idea of happiness the key to a satisfying life? In the same way that people often think of success as a single isolated event rather than a process, many of us fall into the trap of thinking that happiness is something that "just happens" when the conditions in our lives are exactly right. In this chapter, I'm going to take a critical look at the very notion of happiness. **More importantly, I'll also explain why self-discipline is the most reliable path to true contentment.**

According to modern Western standards, happiness can be measured by the number of material possessions you own and the level of prestige you enjoy. Rich celebrities with millions of fans are held up as aspirational figures, regardless of whether they have actually done anything of note. We are taught that a happy life is one that demands minimum effort yet delivers an endless supply of pleasure. Those who can afford to lounge around on yachts all day, free from the constraints of work, are assumed to be the happiest of all. However, research indicates that once you earn enough to cover the basics such as food and rent, there is only a weak link between material wealth and happiness.[6]

You might be surprised to learn that people didn't always assume that living a pleasure-fueled, low-effort lifestyle was the path to fulfilment. **Our modern concept of happiness as the avoidance of pain, together with the maximization of pleasure and safety, only appeared in the 18th century.** In the grand scheme of human history, that's a pretty recent development! If you could travel back in time and ask an ancient Greek whether they agreed with this definition of happiness, they would laugh in your face.

Why? Happiness used to carry very different connotations. **It used to be about achievement, competition, and pride in developing virtues such as generosity and self-control.** Yes, self-discipline used to be seen as the key to happiness! Hard work was revered. No-one aspired to an idle lifestyle. Instead they gained satisfaction from overcoming their weaknesses and working towards a higher ideal, often enduring various ordeals along the way. Does this sound familiar? We're back to the concepts of placing long-term results over instant gratification and making time to work on yourself.

---

[6] Proto, E., & Rustichini, A. (2013). A Reassessment of the Relationship between GDP and Life Satisfaction. *PLoSONE.* http://dx.doi.org/10.1371/journal.pone.0079358

Our attitude towards suffering has also changed over the years. One of the biggest misconceptions Westerners hold about happiness is that it should be available to anyone who wants it, and that we shouldn't have to suffer. **Suffering is seen as the opposite of happiness instead of simply the price we pay for being alive.** We are afraid of suffering, and some of us feel so entitled to a "good life" that we don't see why we ought to put up with anything that gets in the way of what we want.

One of the last remaining taboos in Western society is terminal illness and death. We don't like to acknowledge that we are human and are born with numerous limitations. As a society we are obsessed with remaining young and try to avoid confronting our own mortality at all costs. I've attended several funerals over the past few years, and at no point has anyone matter-of-factly acknowledged that the deceased has actually died. We use euphemisms such as "passed on" and "gone to a better place." These words are uttered with the best of intentions, but they are also very revealing. Few people are truly able to acknowledge the harsh realities of life and death.

Yet suffering is the most natural thing in the world. The wisest people have known this for thousands of years. The Buddha famously noted that life itself is suffering. Everyone is born, everyone suffers, everyone becomes ill, and everyone dies. Buddhism teaches us that we need to accept that pain and discomfort are unavoidable. Almost paradoxically, the greater our acceptance the greater our happiness! Why? **To fully appreciate this teaching, you need to remember that there are in fact two types of suffering.**

The first type of suffering is **necessary suffering**. There is no way of avoiding the most unpleasant parts of human existence such as loss, natural disasters, sickness, and so forth. The second type is **unnecessary suffering.** This stems from rumination, procrastination and avoidance of confrontation with problems. **It is self-generated.** Remember, it isn't just what happens to you that determines your mental state but also how you react.

For example, when you fall ill with the flu, the symptoms of your sickness are necessary suffering. Short of a miracle, you have no option but to wait until they pass. However, if you dwell on the outings you are missing because you are laid up in bed, this crosses the line into the realm of rumination and pointless negativity. Your feelings of sadness and self-pity are not inevitable. **From this perspective, your suffering is unnecessary.**

Procrastination is another kind of unnecessary suffering. Ironically, we often procrastinate because we want to avoid pain or discomfort, yet in doing so we only make the situation worse! For example, suppose you have two weeks in which to write and give a presentation at work. You might be very nervous at the thought of public speaking and have little faith in your ability to put together all the information your boss has included in the brief. Even worse, members of the senior management team will be in attendance.

If you would procrastinate in this situation, you are not alone. Procrastination is often caused by fear, which in turn is often tied to the anxiety we feel when things are out of our control. In this example, you know that to write the presentation will force you to confront the fact that you will soon be standing up in front of a group of people who will be assessing your every move and may even ask you some difficult questions. The prospect of being subjected to such scrutiny might make you feel extremely anxious. Not wanting to suffer through this anxiety, you delay starting on your presentation for another few days.

Most of you know how this story ends – in fact, I've lived it myself in the early days of my career. You end up putting off the dreaded task so long because you are frightened of how it will make you feel **that you actually end up suffering on two levels.** Not only do you still have to confront the original task but you also have to contend with the guilt, regret, and extra stress. Worst of all, you know that if you'd just sat down and made a start at the earliest opportunity, you wouldn't be suffering so much.

This kind of scenario is so common because on some level we believe that we shouldn't have to suffer at all. Yet if we could be brave enough to tell ourselves that fear and suffering is **inevitable** and **we just have to make the most sensible choice** – to suffer now rather than compound the issue and suffer even more later on – **we would be happier**.

Another misconception we tend to hold about happiness is that it's an all-or-nothing state. We tend to think that in order to be happy, we should not only feel positive emotions but also experience a lack of negative feelings such as sadness, uncertainty, and grief. This leads to the typical Western scenario in which we look around at our secure homes, access to clean water, 24/7 entertainment and wonder why we can't "just be happy."

We forget that we are human, and **there is room for us to feel negative emotions along with gratitude and happiness.** Our moods are often subject to variables beyond our control, and sometimes we must accept that there is no immediately obvious reason why we feel the way we do. Have you ever woken up one morning feeling unusually cheerful but then found yourself more downcast a few days later? **This is completely normal, but we tend to forget that not everything needs an explanation. If you make self-discipline a priority, these day-to-day fluctuations won't bother you.** You'll be too busy making sure that you are meeting your goals and obligations.

By now, the limitations of our Western ideas of suffering and happiness should be clear. We cannot hope to become happy by avoiding all suffering, as we often try to do, because some of it is unavoidable. In reality, happiness can only be attained when we manage to avoid the unnecessary suffering. How can we manage this? **Self-discipline!** Self-discipline allows you to be as happy as a person can reasonably hope to be, given that you will inevitably come up against obstacles in every area of your life. Even better, good self-discipline actually helps you find a kind of **enjoyment and pride in overcoming setbacks.** It takes a great deal of bravery to face up to the reality of suffering, but since it is inevitable anyway you may as well resolve to take a rational, balanced view of life in which happiness is an experience to be enjoyed but never taken for granted.

Chapter 8: The Power (And The Traps) Of Positive Thinking

We've all been told that positivity will help us feel happier and be more productive, but it needs to be approached in the right way. Positive thinking can help you achieve your goals, but you need to balance positivity **with action** or else nothing will change in your life.

In this chapter, we're going to look at exactly how you can reap the benefits of a positive attitude without relying on unrealistic optimism or blind faith. You may have noticed that throughout this book I've tried to emphasize how important it is to stay grounded in reality. There is no magic pill, three-day course or perfect self-help book that will do the work that needs to get done. Your success in life is ultimately down to you. **It's about finding a balance between contemplation and action.**

You need to remember that as human beings, we are **always** focusing on **something**. How we choose to focus our attention has a significant impact on how we feel, which in turn can affect our self-discipline and drive. Even people with ADHD always focus on something – it's just that they tend to switch rapidly from one thing to another. Therefore, how you choose to direct your attention is vital. A good first step is to focus on what you have rather than what you lack. This can be done using a simple gratitude exercise. **Every morning or evening, spend a few minutes thinking about all that is great in your life.** Write it down – this is a good exercise in self-discipline and will also help you take the concept of positive thinking and gratitude more seriously. Your list doesn't have to be full of amazing experiences – being grateful for running water and a bed to sleep in is enough. However, the best method is to keep a diary in which you never dwell on all the bad things that happened to you and instead write down all the good situations, emotions and moments you have experienced.

If you aren't actively focusing on the good, you will naturally start to focus on the bad. As humans, we can't concentrate on nothing at all in life. This means you need to make a choice – are you going to think about what's going well, or what's going wrong? **Negativity breeds helplessness and depression**, which will do nothing to move you towards your goals. On the other hand, getting into the habit of concentrating on the positives in your life will serve you well. It will train you to see the world as a place of exciting opportunities.

Note that taking time to feel grateful and positive will give you a boost and help increase your momentum when going after a goal, **but it is by no means a substitute for real action!**

Beware positive thinking philosophies that encourage laziness! Take for example the "Law Of Attraction." For those of you who don't know, the LOA is based on the premise that everything in the universe is made up of vibrations. From there, it speculates that "like attracts like" – for example, water droplets are attracted to other water droplets because they operate at the same frequency. Now here's the kicker – LOA practitioners maintain that humans also vibrate at particular frequencies, and that we attract the people and outcomes that literally resonate with us. According to this reasoning, we are most likely to experience positive outcomes if we think positive thoughts and raise our vibration. Whilst there may be some scientific logic underlying this theory, it has yet to be proven. The important point to note is that all too often, self-help literature based on the LOA fools people into thinking that they can expect great results without actually having to put in any effort. The LOA can provide you with inspiration, but ultimately only you can drive the changes you must make in your life.

Two practical tools you can start using right now are visualization and affirmations. When you create an affirmation, you tell yourself that the situation is already how you want it to be. Affirmations should be positive and in the present tense. For example, "I weigh 150lbs and I'm healthy" is a good affirmation if you are looking to lose weight. "I own a house," "Success and wealth come naturally to me," or "I have plenty of money" are good choices if you are working towards specific financial goals. Repeat your affirmations throughout the day and before falling asleep, writing them down on sticky notes or on your phone as appropriate.

Affirmations work best when accompanied by visualization. Every time you say or read your affirmations, close your eyes and conjure up a convincing mental picture. Imagine what you will feel, touch, taste, see and hear once you have reached your goal. This will trigger a strong emotional state that will make your goal seem real and accessible. Top athletes, actors and military personnel in the Special Forces act and think as though they have already succeeded. **When combined with a practical plan of action and sheer determination, it's a winning formula.** Make sure you know precisely how to achieve your goals before you start using affirmations and visualization, otherwise you'll feel good about yourself but won't actually see your life change.

It's important to remember that positive thinking isn't a magic cure-all. Even the most positive people will still suffer – suffering is inevitable from time to time. Some situations just plain suck. For example, let's say you have a beloved pet dog. Unfortunately, your dog becomes sick. Your vet tells you that your dog can still live for years to come – but only with expensive medication and surgery. Because your dog is so important to you, you make the financial sacrifice required. It takes months of medication changes and several surgeries followed by rehabilitation, but finally your pet seems to be healthy. Tragically, your dog is then hit by a car in a freak accident and dies. In this kind of situation, positive thinking is unlikely to make you feel better. All you can do is allow yourself to feel sad or regretful and then look to the future.

What about positive thinking and failure? Some people find that it's easy to remain positive when things are going well, but as soon as something goes wrong they start to question whether there is any point to remaining positive when they are struggling. The answer is not to ignore failure entirely, but to **approach it effectively** and to avoid dwelling on any repetitive negative thoughts. For example, ruminating on what went wrong and thinking things like *Why can I never do anything right? Why do I fail so often?* and *Why are other people better than me?* is a waste of time and energy. **Truly successful people never allow themselves to wallow in this kind of self-generated misery.** Instead, they analyze what happened, what went wrong, and what they could do better next time.

It might seem unlikely, but you really can train yourself to think differently and stop beating yourself up about what has already happened. You really can remain positive even when you are dealing with failure. Once you have taken the lessons it has to offer you on board, you can even engage in some positive self-deception by telling yourself that the mistake never happened. If you catch yourself thinking about past failures again, tell yourself that it's in the past, that you've learned your lesson, and that it may as well have not happened. That's how many successful athletes and businesspeople move on from even the most spectacular of failures and poor decisions. It's a very effective solution, even though it may feel strange at first.

Be aware that you can go too far in the pursuit of positivity and lose touch completely with your emotions. This may feel good in the short term, but can actually deprive you of valuable opportunities. **When you start deluding yourself that you are much happier than you are,** you lose the access to negative but truly powerful feelings such as frustration, anger, and despair. Although they may hurt, these emotions can serve as a great, long lasting fuel towards change, a fantastic real-life motivator and an effective kick in the butt. For example, frustration and sadness at being made redundant could be just the emotional fuel you need to finally set up your own business or retrain for a career that suits you much better. **When used in the wrong way, positive thinking also encourages you to avoid taking**

practical action that prevents situations from getting worse. Sometimes you need to confront your problems or else they will compound and cause further issues. You need to become skilled in identifying what you can let go, and what you need to tackle in the present. A common example is debt management. Taking a positive attitude towards your debt and looking to short-term solutions such as credit cards rather than facing up to it and devising a realistic plan to pay the money back will only end in disaster. Remember this: **the fewer confrontations you have in life the more complications you will have.** When you gloss over your problems with positivity, you just delay inevitable suffering. However, choosing to face life with a positive outlook will generally benefit you now and in the future.

Chapter 9: Why Failure Is The Key To Success

How does the word "failure" make you feel? Many of us fear failure even more than we fear death! **In this chapter, I'm going to force you to re-examine failure and even embrace it.** You'll learn how we come to fear failure so much in the first place, why you should expect to fail, why it's no bad thing to mess up from time to time, and what you can learn from your mistakes. We fear failure so much for two main reasons. **The first relates to a loss of control.** Even those of us with laid-back personalities like to feel that we know what will happen next. We like to know roughly where we are headed in life, because this gives us a chance to prepare for emotional upheaval or periods of stress. When the unexpected occurs, we are caught off-balance. This is why even "good surprises" such as a lottery win or falling in love with someone we've just met can be so disruptive. With any goal comes the risk of failure. We can never be certain of the outcome, and we can never fully anticipate how we'll feel about success or failure until it actually arrives.

The second reason comes down to social conditioning. From the time we enter kindergarten – or even before – everyone goes out of their way to tell us that failure is the worst thing that can befall a person. If you think about it, this doesn't make a whole lot of sense, because the average child does pretty well by failing! By the time you start junior school you'll have learned to walk, talk and feed yourself. How did you master such an impressive set of skills? By failing, of course. Babies aren't born knowing how to walk. They must first learn how to crawl and then fall over countless times before finally being able to walk more than a few steps. Yet once they are in the school system, they soon learn that unless they understand something the first time around then they are weak and inferior.

As children get older, parents and teachers become even less tolerant of failure. If you think back to your own school days, you'll probably remember that feeling of dread every time parents' evening rolled around or your report card was mailed home. By college, lots of us get upset at the very idea of receiving an average grade for a piece of work or failing a class. Some people become so paralyzed by the prospect of failure that they refuse to engage altogether and drop out, settling for courses and careers far below their true level of ability.

Is it any wonder that as adults we are often so hesitant to make a leap into a potentially risky situation? In my case, fear of failure was definitely a factor that kept me bound to the 9-5 lifestyle for so many years. I know I'm not the only one! Maybe you sometimes imagine living the life of your dreams, working your ideal job for another company or becoming self-employed. But then the fear sets in. You start thinking things like *I know I'm good at my job, but what if I can't make it in a new field? What if I can't find any clients? What if I turn up to networking events and people laugh in my face? Is there any special training I have to do to be self-employed? What if I just run out of motivation? If I ever want to work in my old industry again, would anyone ever hire me?* You can lose hours to these thoughts if you're not careful. **Rumination leads to exhaustion, which saps your motivation to change.** Only when you realize that the fear won't magically vanish will your choice become clear. **You can be afraid and let yourself stay in the same place, or accept it and make the leap anyway.**

There is one simple way to avoid failure, and that's by doing nothing. If you are so certain that you can't handle even minor disasters, then by all means stay in your comfort zone and take no risks. But remember, there's price to pay for everything in life. The price to pay for not taking any chances is steep. Do you really want to pay it? There is every chance that you will come to regret not taking particular opportunities and missing out on fulfilling your ambitions. Risks also give you a sense of adrenalin and even purpose. They are life-enhancing, and to choose a life of safety is to deprive yourself of self-development.

Failure is inevitable, so you may as well get used to the idea that sometimes you will fall flat on your face. This isn't because you are intrinsically stupid or incompetent. It's simply because there are too many variables beyond our control, and because **we must work within our limitations.** This point bears repeating: *You cannot afford to take failure personally.* You can write out the perfect business plan, only to have the economy tank on you during the first year. You can come up with an excellent diet and exercise regimen and break your arm, making your goals null and void. It happens.

What really matters is how you choose to respond to failure. **Just as with everything else in life, you have a choice. It all comes down to how you perceive the situation.** To understand this better, think of the placebo effect. Research in medicine and psychology has shown that if you give a group of people an inactive sugar pill and tell them it is designed to cure a particular problem such as a headache or nausea, the average person is likely to tell you that the medication has helped them feel better! This is why drug companies often run trials that compare the results of a drug with the results of a placebo.[7] In order to learn just how effective a

---

[7] Davies, J. (2014). *Cracked: Why Psychiatry Is Doing More Harm Than Good.* London: Icon Books.

drug is, they need to account for the results that patients would get anyway merely as a result of being given a tablet. The placebo effect shows us that our beliefs are powerful. **A single shift in your perception can trigger meaningful results.** How does this relate to failure? Let's look at two possible ways in which you can react when things go wrong, starting with the most common type of response.

Most people see their failures as confirming their deepest, darkest fears. **The fear that they aren't good enough.** The fear that the world never rewards those who put in hard work. The fear that although other people can get whatever they want, success will always be elusive for them personally. **Much like the placebo effect, it becomes a self-fulfilling prophecy.** The pioneering car manufacturer Henry Ford famously said that whether you believe you can or can't do something, you are right. If you interpret your failures as an accurate reflection on your abilities – or lack thereof – you will kickstart a downward spiral. You will teach yourself that there is no point in even trying because everything is destined to failure. Your self-discipline will hit an all-time low, and success will seem even further away.

There is another way of responding to failure and it's much healthier. The most successful people not only anticipate failure, they welcome it as high-quality fuel that fires up their determination. Once you have failed a few times, you know that you are gathering priceless information about what doesn't work. Therefore, you can think of failure as an information-gathering exercise that will help you eliminate what doesn't work and hone in on the right steps to take in the future.

Everyone who has achieved something great has failed numerous times along the way. This is true in every field you can think of. For example, the author Stephen King has spoken publicly about the disheartening experience of receiving numerous rejection letters before finally having his first novel, *Carrie,* accepted for publication. Since then, he has gone on to sell millions of books in dozens of countries. In business, it isn't uncommon to see your first, second and even third attempts crash and burn.

Failure isn't the opposite of success – it's part of it. Every time you fail and carry on regardless, you become stronger. You prove to yourself and others around you that pain and discomfort doesn't bring you down. The very best part? The more you fail, the better you become at dealing with it. The better you feel about failure, the more you'll feel inclined to try. This is just as well because the bigger the success, the more failures are required! To learn fast, fail often and fail early. Anyone can reach out and grab something within easy reach but it takes true grit and the ability to look failure in the face if you want to soar. Listen to what your failures can teach you, and in the end you'll be glad that you encountered various obstacles along the way to eventual success. Failure doesn't just give you insight into where your practical skillset needs an upgrade. It also helps you build your inner resources.

At this point, you may agree with everything I've said but still feel reluctant to truly accept failure. In the next chapter, I'm going to share with you the basics of a philosophy that helped me come to terms with the fact that not everything is within my control.

Chapter 10: How Zen Philosophy Can Help You Achieve Your Goals

Wouldn't it be wonderful to know that whatever life throws at you, you'll be able to process it and move on? Wouldn't it be great to live free from that underlying anxiety you feel whenever change looms large on the horizon? **What about losing your fear of never having done quite enough with your life, and even feeling comfortable with the inevitability of death?** You're about to learn the basics of an ancient philosophy that has been enriching Eastern lives for thousands of years. In this chapter we're going to look at Buddhist philosophy, with a concentration on Zen. **You'll learn how it can help you develop a greater level of self-discipline and move you closer to achieving your goals.**

Don't worry, this isn't going to turn into a textbook. There are thousands of books that already explain Zen in depth, and I also have written a book on this fascinating subject. There are several different schools of thought within Zen, and the term is used in a number of ways in Eastern cultures. But here's the good news – you don't need to become any kind of scholar to start benefitting from its teachings today. You don't need to become a Buddhist, meditate for hours each morning, or start wearing orange robes. **You just have to appreciate a few essential ideas in order to bolster your self-discipline.**

Over the past couple of decades, researchers in psychology and self-development fields have noticed that Zen practitioners often enjoy good psychological health. Researchers at Penn State University have spent over a decade looking at the effects of practices associated with Zen, including meditation. It turns out that weaving Buddhist principles into your everyday life can lower stress, induce feelings of calm and help you make better decisions.[8]

Zen Buddhists can teach us a lot about delaying gratification, overcoming fear and accomplishing our goals. This lays a powerful foundation for self-discipline. Zen is not in itself a religion. It's best thought of as a kind of experience, a way of life based on the teachings of the Buddha. The closest Japanese term for Zen is "satori," which roughly translates to "first showing" or "flash of inspiration." To experience Zen is to live in the presence, and fully appreciate that everything is connected. This state is said to be extremely hard to put into words, but roughly speaking it

---

[8] Zimmerman, B. (2014). *Zen State: Researchers, students link contemplation with well-being.* news.psu.edu

entails a suspension of the self and ego.

To put Zen philosophy into context, it helps to know a little about the life of Buddha. Several thousand years ago, he began spreading the teachings and observations which had led to his enlightenment. In short, he taught two key ideas. His first idea was that suffering was very much a part of human life. His second was that for the most part, **we bring it on ourselves**. Having left his life of luxury to go out into the world and learn about the true nature of existence, he noted that the majority of people were bound in a state of misery. He eventually concluded that if we are to break free of the endless cycle of birth, suffering and rebirth, we have to stop allowing our minds to grasp onto the illusions and attachments that we tend to hold onto.

These attachments include our very sense of self. For example, when we are with someone else there is no "I" or "you," just two humans who have created the illusion of two separate egos using the power of their own minds. The aim of Buddhism, and of Zen in particular, is to strip away the incessant mind chatter and illusions we hold about the outside world and realize on a deep level that everything is interconnected. There is no "us" and "them," no "in here and "out there." Once we attain this level of insight, the concerns of society – such as acquiring social status and material possessions – will come to matter a whole lot less. Instead, we can focus on moral development and lead a much more balanced life. We'll also save ourselves much unnecessary suffering by **letting go of the notion that external events can make us happy.**

Buddhism encourages living life in the present moment. The past is merely a set of memories and set of interpretations. The future has yet to arrive, and obsessing or worrying about particular outcomes will only lead to pointless mental suffering.

This may sound a bit abstract and spiritual. A couple of examples from everyday life will help you better understand how it all fits together.

Take the issue of self-identity. **Zen teaches us that holding on too tightly to a rigid idea about who you are and what this means is self-limiting and keeps you locked in the same destructive behavior patterns.** When I started reading about Zen for the first time, I soon realized that I had long had a self-image as a high achiever. This sounds like a good problem to have, right? Well yes – in a sense. But if you have a similar self-image, you'll know that it comes at a cost to your mental health. When you are told from an early age that you're smart, grades and career success will become a major focus in your life as a child and then as an adult. This leaves you at risk of stress and burnout.

Worse still, the prospect of failure becomes scarier over time as you cling tighter and tighter to the idea that you are, and must remain, a high achiever. As if that wasn't enough, you fall into the trap of striving for qualifications that don't actually make you happy. Think about it. **Have you become permanently happier with each new accolade or qualification?** Probably not. It's more likely that you have felt increasingly anxious about being "found out" or revealed to be a fraud. By this point, if you experience failure then your self-image will unravel and your world will tip upside down. People hate the possibility that their lives might slide out of control (and I'm not immune to this either).

Incorporating Zen principles and the teachings of Buddha into your life will help you develop self-discipline and ultimately achieve your goals. Why? Firstly, you will accept that since suffering is inevitable, you should be prepared to work for whatever it is you want. Second, you will gain more control over your own mind. Rather than losing hours to pointless rumination and regrets, you'll be busy appreciating what's going on in the present. Most Buddhists advocate meditation for just this purpose, which we will cover in the next chapter. Third, you will feel less constrained by fear. After all, fear is just an inevitable result of thinking about all the potential ways in which things could go wrong. If you don't allow your mind to dwell on all the negative possibilities, fear will no longer hold you back. Your thought processes will be sharper and you will be calmer, because you will no longer be fighting against a flood of negative thoughts.

Now let's go back to the issue of goals. You'd be forgiven for thinking that if Buddhism encourages you to dissolve the boundaries between your ego and the world around you whilst refusing to dwell on the future, there's little room left for setting and working towards goals. Yet this isn't the case. The Buddha himself outlined a spiritual framework known as The Eightfold Path, which includes guidelines such as "right speech," "right view," and "right action." Not only are these guidelines distinctly proactive in themselves – you can't get much more proactive than "right action"– but they are definitely goals. Therefore, there is no contradiction between adding the central ideas of Zen into your life whilst looking to improve it at the same time.

There's an added bonus that comes when you live in the present. When you think about the distance between where you currently are and where you'd like to be, it's easy to feel demotivated. You start thinking about what you lack, and the journey ahead feels daunting. **When you focus on taking things one step at a time, you'll be thinking about the next small mini-goal rather than a distant end result. This stops you feeling overwhelmed by your "bigger vision."**

So how can you train yourself to think and act like a Zen Buddhist? In the next chapter I'm going to tell you exactly how some of the most disciplined people on the planet use Buddhist principles to meet their goals and push themselves further than most of us would ever dream possible.

Chapter 11: Mastering Self-Discipline The Shaolin Way

Now that you understand the key ideas behind Zen and how you can use them to achieve your goals, it's time to look at how this can work in practice. We're going to look at the habits and lifestyle of a special group of Buddhist monks – the Shaolin. By examining their day-to-day routines and beliefs, you'll soon understand how following the principles you learned in the last chapter can lay the foundations for a life of self-discipline. Even better, Shaolin monks enjoy greater overall wellbeing and a sense of inner peace! It's no wonder that their lifestyle has gradually become an inspiration for many Westerners.

So, who exactly are these exceptional individuals? The Shaolin Monastery in China is one of the most famous Zen Buddhist temples in the world. According to legend, it was founded approximately 1500 years ago when a Buddhist teacher known as Buddhabhadra travelled from India all the way to China. His revolutionary idea was that the core teachings of Buddhism could be passed from a master to student.[9] Until that point, Buddhist monks had usually relied on scriptures and written interpretations. Buddhabhadra's idea impressed the Chinese Emperor, who allocated to him the funds required to build a new temple. The monks were not only trained in spiritual discipline, but also became renowned for their fighting skills. They are taught over 70 special moves including the famous "Iron Head" technique. Those who have perfected this exercise are capable of breaking concrete slabs using just their foreheads. The monks' skills are so impressive that they sometimes tour the world, giving demonstrations to large audiences.

Today, despite numerous attacks and demolitions throughout history, the temple is still home to monks who are famous for their mastery of kung fu. The monks' day starts at 5am and ends at 11pm, with their time split across three main activities – the study of Buddhism, the practicing of kung fu, and essential temple activities such as cleaning and preparing food. Each monk must therefore spend hours each day on grueling physical exercise along with intense mental and

---

[9] Szczepanski, K. (2015). *History of the Shaolin Monks.* thoughtco.com

spiritual training. Their lifestyle allows for few material possessions and outside interests. Upon joining the temple, each monk is required to shave their head as a sign of their allegiance to the teachings of the Buddha and a symbol of their willingness to give up their attachment to material possessions.

So how do they maintain the high level of self-discipline required to stick to such a strict schedule? According to British-born monk Matthew Ahmet, who trained at the temple for several years, the Shaolin hold a set of attitudes very different to those held in the west.[10] For a start, the monks live with access to only the most basic of facilities, washing their clothes by hand and going without running water. This makes them grateful for even the simplest things in life. **This gratitude gives them a positive baseline to work with – when you take time to appreciate the small things, you build psychological momentum.** You begin to believe that the world is fundamentally a good place laden with opportunity, which spurs you on to achieve your goals.

Second, the monks know that material possessions and wealth are not the magic key to happiness. They aren't envious of those living "normal" lives because during their training they come to appreciate that **real contentment and peace comes from finding a passion or mission.** In their case, it's the spiritual and physical progress they make during their time at the temple. This lesson is simple yet powerful – **once you find a goal that aligns with your values and ambitions, your passion will carry you a long way.** Even when times get hard and it feels as though you still have a long way to go, a sense of purpose can shore up your self-discipline.

Third, they do not believe in pushing themselves to the point of pain or injury. Historically, the monks had to be fit and ready to fight at all times in the event of an attack on their temple. They believed that a monk who was ill or injured as a result of too much physical or mental exertion would be no good in battle. This attitude is still upheld by the modern temple inhabitants. Although the monks spend hours each day in physical training, they also take care to include rest periods in their schedule. **They understand that being busy doesn't necessarily equate to being productive. They are taught that sometimes you need to slow down before you burn out.** This is where meditation comes in. Ahmet believes that this is the best way to reduce mind chatter, increase your psychological strength, and learn to

---

[10] Whiting, K. (2015). *11 life-changing secrets of Shaolin monks.* home.bt.com

balance hard work with downtime.

The monks spend hours every day on meditative practices. According to kung fu practitioners, it is important to regulate your emotions and avoid giving into negative impulses. To fight effectively, they believe you must learn how to harness your essential life force. In the Shaolin tradition this is referred to as "chi." Translated from the Chinese, it may mean "air," "energy" or "temper" in English.[11] Monks train for years not only in the high-energy art of kung fu, but they also practice a slow martial art called tai chi. Tai chi is comprised of a collection of physical actions requiring immense concentration and balance. It was developed in order to teach those wishing to learn physical combat how to remain aware and focused in the moment in order to strike quickly and effectively. Shaolin monks attribute their unusual physical toughness, resilience and resistance to injury to this mastery of chi. For example, after a few years of training a typical Shaolin monk will be able to withstand blows to the abdomen and internal organs which would be fatal to anyone else. They use their ability to handle and redirect energy to repel blows and remain uninjured.

Along with granting you the ability to master your chi and quieten your mind, **meditation also helps you get in touch with who you really are.** This is the most important step in discovering your inner passion and purpose. The Shaolin monks find it easy to get up and go about their day with vigor, because **they know exactly what they are going to do and why they are doing it.** This inner conviction drives them to physical, mental and spiritual excellence. Although meditation is often thought of as single experience or practice, for Shaolin monks it is a way of life. They aspire to live a life of continual mindfulness and to retain the highest level of concentration at all times.

It should be clear by now that the Shaolin actually have plenty in common with Navy SEALs. Although their day-to-day activities are very different, each monk and SEAL is strongly allied to their particular cause. They all show immense self-discipline and are willing to give up their regular comforts in order to achieve a greater goal. Just as the SEALs don't wake up raring to go each and every morning, the monks probably don't always feel like training for most of the day. However, with such strong ideals and a strict routine to follow, they never need to rely on feeling "motivated." They know how to cultivate a sense of momentum and seeing their skills increase

---

[11] Cheung, W. (2013). *The Nature and Origins of Chi Power in Wing Chun Kung Fu Training.* blackbeltmag.com

spurs them on still further.

Although their lifestyle sets them apart from almost everyone else on the planet, the Shaolin monks do share one habit in common with most productive people – they have a daily routine and they stick to it. In the next part of the book, I've dedicated a whole chapter to schedules, and how to put together a killer routine that will boost your self-discipline. But before we get there, we're going to learn another practical skill straight from the Shaolin – meditation. Turn to the next chapter to discover how you can start using this ancient spiritual tool in your life right now.

PART II

Chapter 12: Meditation For Focus & Self-Discipline

The previous chapter should have convinced you that regular meditation is an excellent way to increase your self-discipline. If it can produce amazing results for Shaolin monks, imagine what it could do for you!

In this chapter, I'll take you through a couple of basic exercises that will soon set help you become skilled in the art of meditation. If you've ever thought about meditation but then dismissed it as a waste of time or too boring, get ready to rethink your assumptions.

For a start, you don't even have to stay seated for hours each day to meditate "properly." Remember how the Shaolin monks see meditation as a lifestyle rather than a practice? You need to adopt a similar attitude. Sure, you'll benefit most from a regular practice, but the real magic of meditation comes when the ordinary stresses of daily life no longer seem like such a big deal. We'll get into specific techniques shortly, but first I'll spell out exactly how and why meditation is going to help you.

Meditation increases your capacity for making rational decisions and your ability to remain focused on the task at hand. You will also become an expert in delaying instant gratification in favor of what you most want in the long term. Doesn't that sound like a great recipe for self-discipline? The regular hassles of daily life won't suddenly disappear, but they will begin to seem much more manageable. Remember, it isn't what happens to you in life that determines the ultimate outcome but how you react. **Meditation trains you to respond to even the most disheartening of setbacks with a calm, rational outlook.**

Still feeling skeptical? **You'll be pleased to know that there's plenty of scientific evidence in favor of meditation.** For example, a study published in the journal PNAS shows that you can expect to see results in less than a week. The researchers behind the study asked 40 undergraduate students to take part in 20 minutes of meditation training over a five-day period. They were then given a range of psychological tests. Compared to people who hadn't taken part in the training program, the participants were significantly better at directing their attention to one particular task. They were also less fatigued, reported less stress, and were less anxious than the control sample.[12] **Think how much more you could get done if you felt more energized and more in control of your thoughts!** Even when you don't feel motivated to get started on a task, the skills you learn through meditation will enable you to get the job done. **This is the very essence of self-discipline.**

Here's how to get started. First of all, you're going to learn a simple seated meditation. Read these instructions through a few times before your first try, so that you can concentrate fully on what you are doing. You first need to take up an appropriate position. You can adopt a traditional lotus pose if you wish, but sitting cross-legged on the floor or just upright in a comfortable chair is fine. Don't do this whilst lying in bed though or else you risk falling asleep! This won't do you any harm, but to reap the benefits of meditation you do have to remain awake. Incidentally, this meditation practice is known as "Zazen" or simply "Zen meditation," and is regularly practiced by Shaolin monks.

Once you have found a position that is comfortable for you, make sure that your back is straight but not rigid. Keep your mouth closed but not clamped shut, and ensure that your eyes remain open. You should not be staring, but keeping your gaze soft and focused on the floor approximately two feet away.

Now that you have the physical aspect of the meditation sorted out, it's time to focus your mind. There are two techniques you can use here. Experiment with both and see which works best. First, pay attention to your breathing. This forces you to stay in the present moment and quietens your mental chatter. Feel the sensation of air moving through your nose as you inhale, and then out through your mouth as you exhale. Breathe deeply from your stomach rather than your chest. Many Westerners have taught themselves to breathe in a "shallow" way, which reduces oxygen flow and leads to feelings of fatigue. In Buddhism and other Eastern traditions, proper breathing is regarded as an essential practice. **It allows energy to flow properly through the body. Whether or not you believe in the concept of "chi" as a life force, breathing properly is definitely important for good overall health.** If you suffer from panic attacks, learning how to control your breathing can be very helpful. The next time you feel a sense of panic or overwhelming anxiety, focus on slowly drawing air in through your nose and out through your

---

[12] Tang, Y., Ma, Y., Wang, J., Fan, Y., Feng, S., Lu, Q., Yu, Q., Sui, D., Rothbart, M.K., Fan, M., & Posner, M.I. (2007). Short-term meditation training improves attention and self-regulation. *PNAS, 104 (43)*, 17152-17156.

mouth. This helps your body balance its oxygen levels, which in turn will help you feel better. The second technique is known as "Shikantaza," which roughly translates to "just sitting" in English.[13] Most new practitioners find this more difficult than the breathing exercise described above, so don't panic if it seems almost impossible on the first few attempts.

Simply sit and observe what is going on around you, and what is going on within you. If you're like most people (including me), you'll find that your mind is a noisy place. When you take a moment to stop and just pay attention to whatever it is you are thinking about, you'll be amazed at how much mental junk you have. **The aim is not to pass judgment on whatever it is you are thinking about, but to accept each thought before letting it go.** Imagine your thoughts as clouds passing by in the sky – they are there, you can't make them vanish, but you can choose to watch them float past rather than get caught up in what they mean. Once you can do this during meditation sessions, you will start to adopt a healthier attitude towards your negative thoughts in everyday life. Instead of becoming bogged down in unhelpful thoughts such as *I can't do this* and *Everyone is better than me,* you'll be able to let them go and channel your energy into productive activities. Not only will you be a happier and more positive person, but you will no longer waste time on pointless self-deprecation. Taking charge of your mind will leave you feeling empowered.

Whether you are focusing on your breath or "just sitting," you are bound to find that your mind wants to wander from time to time. You may start to think things like *This is dumb* or *I have so many thoughts, how will this ever work?* Don't let yourself get caught up in the mental debris. As soon as you notice that you have started engaging with your thoughts or have lost focus, bring your attention back to the present. There's no need to berate yourself – after all, that's just inviting more mental chatter! Like all skills, meditation gets easier with time. If you've been living the typical multi-tasking Western lifestyle for decades, it's unreasonable to expect that you'll achieve inner peace overnight. **On the other hand, you can realistically expect to feel calmer and more in control of your life and emotions within a few days. Isn't that an exciting thought?**

If you really struggle to sit still for more than a couple of minutes or have such high anxiety levels that you cannot bear to face your own thoughts, try a dynamic form of meditation instead. Zen walking meditation, known as "Kinhin," can be used together with or as an easier alternative to

---

[13] Giovanni. (2016). *Types Of Meditation – An Overview Of 23 Meditation Techniques.* liveanddare.com

seated methods.[14] Remove your shoes and socks, then begin by assuming a standing pose. Keep your posture upright, but do not allow your back to stiffen. Do not rock back and forth on your feet. You should feel grounded, with your weight distributed evenly. Bring your left thumb in towards your palm, and fold your fingers so they are wrapped around it. Now place your left hand lightly against your stomach, just above your naval. Take your right hand and place it on top of your left. Your gaze should be soft and concentrated on the ground approximately six feet away from your body.

Starting with your right foot, take a single step forward every time you breathe in and out. This is a slow practice – only move your foot once you have completed an inhalation-exhalation cycle. Aim for a controlled, smooth movement as you walk around in a clockwise direction. It takes enormous self-discipline to keep your pace even. To an outsider, this exercise may seem peculiar and pointless. However, it is actually a brilliant way of developing some serious self-control. Every time you perform this meditation, you prove to yourself that you can exert total mastery over your movements. This translates into a stronger, more proactive mental attitude that will enhance success in every area of your life. **No wonder some of the most successful businesspeople including Russell Simmons (CEO of Def Jam) and Jeff Weiner (CEO of LinkedIn) make time to meditate on a daily basis.[15]**

So how often should you meditate, and for how long at a time? I personally meditate for 20 minutes in the morning before starting work for the day, and then 20 minutes in the afternoon. I started with 10 minutes twice a day, and built it up by a couple of minutes until two or three days. I prefer seated to walking meditation, but that's just what works best for me.

Even if I have an urgent project demanding my attention, I'd no sooner miss my meditation practice than miss brushing my teeth. It's an essential part of my self-care routine. Without it, I quickly become frazzled and overwhelmed. From now on, your meditation practice is non-negotiable. It's part of your life, because you are a self-disciplined individual who takes their personal growth seriously. I never say that I "try" and meditate every morning – I simply get up and do it. In the next chapter, you'll discover why "trying" at anything is bad news.

---

[14] Giovanni. (2016). *Ultimate Guide to Walking Meditation.* liveanddare.com
[15] Neal, B. (2016). *8 Super-Successful People Who Meditate Daily.* pakwired.com

Chapter 13: Why You Should Say Goodbye To "Try"

One of the simplest yet most powerful practical steps you can take right now in boosting your self-discipline is to remove a single word from your vocabulary. This one change will alter how you see yourself, and greatly increase your self-esteem. It isn't just how you think that shapes the way you live. The words you use, both aloud and in your head, dictate your self-image and ultimately your success.

So what word do you need to cut? From now on, you are no longer going to use the word "try." In this chapter, you'll come to understand why allowing yourself to merely "try" rather than do will hold you back from achieving your goals and undermine your self-discipline at the same time. "Try" may be a little word, but it can cause you big trouble!

Most of us were encouraged to try our best as children. Well-meaning parents and teachers may have reassured us that as long as we put in a decent day's work, the end results didn't matter too much. Popular sayings such as "It's not the winning, but the taking part that counts" and "Well, at least you tried" reinforce this attitude even further. This sentiment is cosy and reassuring. It suggests that there's always a next time, and that there's always another opportunity to succeed. Unfortunately, the harsh truth is that sometimes you don't get another chance to hit your target. You have to seize the moment or lose it forever. Real life just doesn't give us chance after chance! **From now on, you are not going to try. You are going to simply DO.** If you catch yourself saying "I'm going to try..." then stop! Instead say "I'm going to do..." You need to have courage and be decisive in both your speech and your actions. Not only will you come to respect yourself more, but others will start to regard you as a proactive winner rather than someone who is afraid to risk failure and as a result does nothing. When you resign yourself to trying rather than expecting yourself to actually come out on top, you are writing yourself off. **You make yourself smaller.** Rather than assuming that you are going to achieve whatever it is you set your mind to, you fall into the trap of thinking that as long as you try, things will work out somehow. From time to time, you might have luck on your side. Sometimes fate intervenes and everything does fall into place. However, as a general rule you get out of life what you put in. You'll always get better results from taking action than merely trying.

Try comes in various shades of gray, which means you are less likely to hold yourself accountable when you aim to try rather than do. **When you set out to try, you are allowing yourself a lot of wriggle room.** How hard, exactly, do you have to try before you can say that you really gave it your all? **It's hard to measure, isn't it?** This leaves you vulnerable to self-deception. **You end up telling yourself that you tried when in actual fact you merely made a half-assed effort.** On the other hand, if you actually DO, it's clear for you and others to see. It's simple – did you go forth and get the job done or not? There's no room for excuses. You have to use your self-discipline, and work for the results.

To DO, you need to trust in yourself and your abilities. Take an honest inventory of your skills, strengths and weaknesses. This in itself is an act of self-discipline, because it takes guts to face up to who and what you really are. Do not indulge in self-flagellation – that's a waste of time and will just encourage a "poor me" attitude. This won't get you anywhere. If you know that you are capable of succeeding, go out there and do it. If you know that you are going to need help from other people or will need to pick up some new skills first then that's fine too – go out and DO that!

You also need to fully believe that what you are doing will move you closer to your goals. This requires some effort and reflection, but by this point you should have accepted that anything valuable demands hard work. Before you embark on a new project, ask yourself what it is you are really trying to achieve. **Don't just sit there and think about it – take out a pen and piece of paper and make a list.** If you aren't quite sure of your aims, don't get started until you know exactly where you want to end up. Otherwise you'll waste precious time and energy. Without proper planning, you also run the risk of developing a self-image as someone who always tries yet fails time and time again. **This sets off a vicious circle in which you lose your confidence, so feel less able to attack new projects, which leads to further disappointment, and so forth.** The solution is to choose your goals wisely, weigh up your chances of success, and then strike! **Trying is messy.** Doing is clean, assertive and decisive.

Telling yourself that you are going to try rather than do is to immediately focus on limitations and obstacles rather than possibilities. This naturally leads to negative, unhelpful beliefs that will hold you back. For example, let's say you want to lose weight. You tell yourself that you will try to stick to your diet and try to squeeze in a few workouts every week so that you can lose those 20lbs that have crept on over the past few years. The problem here is that you are already setting yourself up for a struggle. You are allowing yourself to dwell on the possibility that you will expend a huge amount of time and effort only to miss out on the end result. The assumption that you are going to try to lose weight rather than actually manage to get lean encourages unhelpful thoughts such as *I'll try to resist temptation but it's so hard, I'll try to exercise but it takes up too much time* and *I'm always trying to lose weight, but it always comes back.* This style of thinking isn't going to give you the healthy push you need to achieve your goals, is it?

Of course, whatever it is you are attempting will either work out or fail. If you succeed, then great! On the other hand, if you are afraid of failure, the prospect of your project falling flat will terrify you. If you haven't come to terms with the power and benefits of failure, go back to Chapter 9 for a refresher. Trying doesn't really build character, but taking action and learning from the end result certainly does. Failure really isn't the end of the world. Far worse is living a life of half-hearted attempts and a lack of self-discipline.

Successful people know that in order to get anything done, they must assume that they will meet their goals and continually push themselves harder. They act rather than try. For example, the renowned self-development expert, author and speaker Deepak Chopra is well-known for his productivity and energy. He is famous for his contribution to the New Age movement and is also a successful entrepreneur, having amassed a multi-million dollar fortune. To date, he has written over 15 books. At the age of 69 he still works full-time and regularly embarks on speaking tours around the world. When asked how he finds the time to continue expanding his publishing empire despite numerous other demands in his life, Chopra has been quoted as saying "Don't try. Do."[16]

Aside from imposing a ban on phrases like "I'm trying…" and "I want to try…," how else can you make this mental shift? You need to shore up your self-belief. **Give yourself some momentum by setting yourself targets that you are almost certain to achieve**. For example, setting yourself the goal of exercising for five minutes every morning is highly achievable and will allow you to prove that you have the beginnings of self-discipline. Remember that self-talk is key. Once you have decided on your first achievable goal, remind yourself several times a day that you are going to DO it.

What else will help you do rather than try? Habits and routines that cultivate success. When you know **what you are going to do and how you will get there,** you become a doer rather than someone who merely tries. In the next chapter, I'll explain why winning and losing are both habits, and how with a few simple rules you can put yourself firmly on the path to regular and ongoing victory.

---

[16] Dawson, J. (2016). *Don't Try. Do.* iamgenie.org

Chapter 14: The Only Rules of Training You'll Ever Need

You'll get the most from life when you start viewing it like a training academy. Life is a dynamic, ever-changing experience that demands discipline and self-awareness if you are to reach your full potential. Even when you meet your goals, there's no time to stand still. Pause for too long and you'll run out of momentum. It all comes back to the choices you make. **You don't get to opt out – you are always training yourself in one direction or the other. You can train towards a winning mindset, or a losing mindset.** It's about taking responsibility for your life direction. In this chapter, we'll look at five basic rules which will help you excel at anything you desire.

These rules will help you succeed in any area of your life. Whether you want to become more efficient at work, find a healthier relationship or shift some weight the principles are exactly the same. Once you have them mastered, your productivity will soar along with your self-belief. The rules provide you with a useful framework that promotes self-discipline and responsibility. It isn't easy, but it's worth it. As you read through this chapter, think about how you can apply them to a goal or ambition you are currently pursuing.

The first rule is to know precisely what you want. I touched on this in the last chapter, but it warrants a little more explanation here. Before you embark on any project there are two questions you must be able to answer. First, can you describe in detail what it is that you want?

The more detailed your vision, the better your chances of success. Going after a vaguely defined goal is not particularly inspiring. Consider these two statements - "I'm going to lose 15lbs" versus "I'm going to lose 15lbs, double the weight I can lift in the gym, and buy three fantastic new outfits once I achieve my goal by the end of July!" Which sounds more exciting? The latter is a much better approach because it inspires more emotion and is much more specific. We humans are emotion-driven creatures, so why not make the most of it?

Here's the second question - can you explain why it is you want this particular outcome so badly? **Pursuing a goal for the sake of it won't get you far. You need to have a bigger vision.** Ideally, a goal should align with your ultimate purpose and core values in life. For example, let's say your goal is to write a 50,000-word book based on your experiences in the business world. For most people, this would be a huge challenge. However, let's say that you've always valued education and want to make this book accessible to a wide audience including those who never got the opportunity to go to business school or have never had the chance to gain any business experience. From this perspective, your mission is in line with your core values. This underlying purpose can keep you going even on those days you feel too tired or distracted to write and would rather watch TV instead.

You should also consider what you are going to have to sacrifice in pursuit of your goal. Remember, pain and suffering is inevitable and the rule still applies when you are chasing your dreams! Anything worthwhile is going to demand that you give up something. For example, if you want to get fit then you might have to get up earlier in the morning and make time to work out. If you want to meet a financial goal such as accumulating a certain amount of money, you may have to stick to a budget. Get realistic about what you are going to have to give up, and you won't be in for any nasty surprises further down the line. **What's more, this exercise also forces you to consider whether what you want is really worth the sacrifice.** On one hand, we tend to value what we've had to work for, so it's no bad thing to endure some pain! However, if you weigh up the pros and cons and decide that the sacrifice isn't worth the end result then it's time to reassess your goals.

The second rule is to approach your goal in a straight line. Again, we are back to doing rather than trying. People who merely try tend to attempt to solve a problem or meet a goal via numerous means. They often put in only the bare minimum because part of them thinks that if they fail, they can always try something else! This is grossly inefficient. You need to get into the habit of clarifying the steps you must take to reach your goal, double-checking the details, and then deciding to get it done. **It's well worth taking an hour or two to set out your plan in some depth.** Your plan may have to change if you come up against any unforeseen obstacles, but you need a reliable starting point. A good plan can spur you on when things are tough, because it acts as a reminder that the journey does have an end point and that you have made sure that your goal is realistic.

The third rule is to focus on taking small steps day by day. Strange as this may seem, taking small steps can require just as much self-discipline as huge strides. When you first start out on a journey, it's tempting to make as much headway as possible in a short period of time. The initial burst of motivation can make you feel as though you can achieve anything, so you channel all your energy into making progress. Unfortunately, as we all know, you cannot rely on motivation alone. **Do so and you risk burning out.** You may even become despondent when the inevitable crash happens. The solution is to follow your plan to the letter. If you feel especially excited and motivated it's fine to enjoy the feeling, but it's more helpful in the long run to

develop the habit of working at a sensible, measured pace. Keep a logbook or diary and use it to record your progress. In a few weeks or months from now, you'll be proud of yourself for maintaining a steady pace. It will stand as solid proof that you are a highly disciplined individual, and this will push you to chase your next dream!

The fourth rule of training states that you win only when you work out what it is you need to do and then repeat it as necessary. Let's say your goal is to be fluent in Spanish. Specifically, you want to be able to understand a Spanish newspaper. How would repetition come into play here? If you want to learn a new language, you need to figure out which exercises and drills you can do which will help you master vocabulary, spelling and grammar. This may mean downloading a couple of apps to your phone, buying a book of exercises, or getting any other tools you are going to need. Then you need to commit to repeating the exercises once, twice or even three times each day depending on how quickly you need to reach your goal. Sometimes you may feel bored, but this is the price you pay for success. **It's fine to feel frustrated on occasion – just get it done. If you miss a day, don't waste time and energy beating yourself up or making excuses.** Pick up where you left off and vow to stick to your plan going forward.

The final rule is to pay attention to the small victories along with your end goal. For example, let's say that you want to improve your fitness and run a full marathon. If you don't currently get much exercise, that will seem like a huge goal. If you think about the end result too much you will soon become dispirited and perhaps give up altogether. **A better approach is to look forward to celebrating every time you meet a new sub-goal such as running five kilometres without stopping, then ten, and so on.** This gets you into the habit of winning and pushing yourself to victory. **Triumph then becomes a habit, and your self-image as a winner will be strengthened even further.**

Whatever your goal, remember that you always get more of whatever you focus on. When you believe that you are capable of achieving your desired end result, victory will be yours provided that you take consistent action. This is why maintaining a positive attitude and self-image is so important. Think of yourself as a winner, and that's exactly what you will become! Undertaking a grueling quest towards a goal can soon deplete your energy – if you haven't braced yourself for the hard work required. In the next chapter, I'll tell you why it's vital that you learn to enjoy the process of chasing a goal.

Chapter 15: Falling In Love With The Process

Once you've identified your goal and worked out what you need to do in order to get there, the next step is to train yourself to enjoy the process. Why? Because if you rely on either motivation or sheer grit to see you through, you won't last long. In this chapter, I'll teach you how to actually enjoy putting in the kind of hard work you'll need to do in order to fulfil your potential.

We've already discussed the limitations of motivation. Focusing on a goal can be highly empowering and drive you forward, but the day-to-day grind involved in actually getting there can sap your energy unless you train yourself to enjoy the work involved. **Fortunately, with a basic knowledge of psychology you too can actually look forward to the journey as much as the destination.**

If you've ever trained an animal, you will already know about the power of association. One of the most famous figures in psychology, Ivan Pavlov, demonstrated this way back in the 1890s.[17] Pavlov was technically a physiologist by training, but his findings still have huge implications for how we understand behavior today. He was interested in how dogs salivated when they were being fed. However, over time he noticed something interesting – the dogs began to salivate when they heard Pavlov's assistant walking down the corridor or entering the room, even when he wasn't carrying any food.

Pavlov realized that the dogs had come to associate the sound of the footsteps with food, which triggered an automatic salivation response. He then built on this work by ringing a bell just before feeding the dogs. After a few days, the dogs began drooling whenever he rang the bell.

How is this relevant to 21st-century humans? Because it shows that instead of having to force particular responses, we can harness the power of conditioning instead. If you can pair a difficult or unpleasant task with positive feelings, over time the task will actually become enjoyable because your mind will have formed a positive association between action and feeling. Imagine what it would be like to feel happy at the prospect of hard work! It's entirely possible.

This needn't be a complicated process. You merely have to think about ways in which you can trigger feelings of pleasure and calm before, during and immediately after a task. **When you implement them on a consistent basis, the process will begin to seem much easier.**

For example, suppose you want to start your own business. In order to do so, you need to put

---

[17] McLeod, S. (2013). *Pavlov's Dogs.* simplypsychology.org

together a business plan before the bank will grant you a loan. You know that this will take many hours of research, writing and fact-checking and the very thought of sitting down at your computer fills you with dread. What could you do to form the kind of positive associations that will see you through the hardest and most complicated aspects of the job?

Here are a few ideas to get you started. Before sitting down to work, you could pour a glass or mug of your favorite drink. After a few days, your mind will have paired the pleasurable sensations generated by ingesting the drink with work. Alternatively, you could spend a few minutes reading an inspiring article or even taking an invigorating shower complete with your favorite gel or soap. This will encourage you to pair a particular scent and temperature with productive work.

Whilst working, you could play some pleasant sounds in the background. Music with lyrics is too distracting for most people, but ambient noise that appeals to you such as coffee shop sounds or rainfall are often calming. Even when your work is difficult, you will still be able to enjoy a feeling of serenity and condition yourself to feel positive whenever you work on the project. You will come to associate these noises with productivity, and therefore set into motion a self-reinforcing cycle. **When you finish a session, you should also give yourself a reward that you associate only with this particular project.** For example, you could allow yourself to watch an episode of a new TV series only once you have completed a particular task. Note that this isn't just using a simplistic reward system. You are training your brain to form a link between working hard and experiencing positive emotions to the point where after a while you won't even need the reward. **The association will be so strong that the grind will be its own payoff.**

To give another example, let's say you want to work out more often at the gym in order to lose a specific amount of weight. You could put together a playlist of songs you really like and only allow yourself to listen to them whilst working out. Immediately you have an incentive to go to the gym, and as you come to associate the music with working out the latter will feel more pleasurable in and of itself. You will find that even if you forget your phone or MP3 player one day, you will still feel inclined towards working out.

This process demonstrates the power of the subconscious mind in action. When you repeat a behavior over and over again, **you no longer have to waste precious time and energy debating whether you should or shouldn't do something. You just get on with it.**

Another powerful method that will help you begin to love the process is to tap into your sense of identity. **When you achieve your goals, what type of person will you have become?**

Thinking of yourself as a person undergoing a transformation can restore your faith in the day-to-day grind and help you see it as an exciting time of change rather than a long hard slog. For example, if you are training for a marathon then think of yourself not as someone who is working towards a certain event but as someone who is in the process of becoming the type of person who cares about their health, who is full of energy, and doesn't feel daunted at the prospect of a physical challenge. Remember that whatever you visualize and imagine you can achieve, as long as you are willing to put in the time and effort required. **How would you like to feel about yourself? It's empowering to realize that the only thing standing between where you currently are and how you'd like to be is consistent action.**

One of the smartest ways of thinking about the process of working towards your goals is to feel grateful that you have the opportunity in the first place. So many people lack the time, energy and imagination needed to dream of a better life and kickstart the process of self-growth. Just before you start your training session or sit down to work on a project, take a moment to feel glad and excited that you have the ability to change your life through your own efforts. Every time you complete a sub-goal, give yourself a reward. You need to train your mind to anticipate rewards, pleasure and positive feelings every step of the way as you move towards your ultimate goal. **It may sound silly or childish, but simply writing down what you did on a particular day and even giving yourself a gold star on a calendar can spur you on.**

A gold star may not serve much purpose in and of itself, but the symbolism is powerful. Noticing a long line of stars on a calendar every time you pass it in the kitchen or office will remind you how rewarding the process can be, even if you still have a way to go before reaching your goal. You can also try using applications such as "Habitica." It "gamifies" your everyday tasks and habits, thus making the process more rewarding.

On the other hand, sometimes we fall into the trap of forgetting that periods of grueling work are inevitable and necessary. We may also think that no-one else struggles as much as we do. **This is usually because we compare our private behind-the-scenes battles with others' public triumphs.** We all know those who appear to "have it all" without expending too much effort, and we all see stories in the media of so-called "overnight successes" in the entertainment industry. What we don't see is the endless hours of practice, sweat, grind and hustle that go into the final outcome. Rest assured that anyone who has ever achieved widespread acclaim or success has had to put in a lot of hard work. This realization can be enough to strengthen your resolve, because once you accept that the path to victory is long and challenging you can stop wasting your energy putting up resistance and work on learning how to love the process instead. Along with an ability to enjoy the work required to achieve your goals, you also need to train yourself to avoid giving into distractions and temptations that could throw you off course. In the next chapter, we'll look at the scientific research behind temptation and how you can learn to delay gratification.

Chapter 16: Delaying Gratification & Overcoming Temptation

Learning how to delay gratification and overcome the desire to see instant results is one of the key skills you will need to grow your self-discipline. Once you've mastered the art of focusing on what you want most rather than what you want in the present, the chances that you will achieve your goals shoot up. In this chapter, I'll give you some simple tricks and tips to enhance your self-control, delay gratification and resist temptation. Note that "simple" doesn't always mean "easy." Self-control is much like a muscle and the more often you practice the art of delayed gratification, the easier it becomes. Not only that, but you'll find yourself actively choosing to make progress on long-term projects rather than getting sidetracked by distractions such as the internet.

We all know people who seem to have laser-like concentration. Once they know what needs to be done, they get on with the task in hand and don't allow themselves to do anything else until it's complete. At the other end of the spectrum, you probably have a couple of friends or relatives who never knuckle down and make progress on any project because their attention wanders. Research suggests that these differences show up early in life. The most famous experiment in this area is probably the marshmallow test carried out by Walter Mischel over 40 years ago.[18]

Mischel and his colleagues devised a simple setup that allowed them to investigate self-control and the ability to delay gratification in young children. Preschoolers were each presented with a plate containing two marshmallows. Next to the plate Mischel would place a bell. Each participant was told that the researcher had to leave the room for a few minutes. Whilst the researcher was gone, the child could make a choice – to wait until they came back and earn themselves both marshmallows, or ring the bell to summon the researcher back and only be allowed to eat one marshmallow.

Mischel tracked the same children down years later. By this point they had reached adolescence. It turned out that the children who were able to delay gratification as preschoolers turned into teenagers who were more likely to earn higher grades, be rated as more resilient to stress by parents and teachers, and show enhanced ability to concentrate compared with those who had caved and eaten the single marshmallow all those years before. But the experiment didn't end there. Mischel caught up with the subjects yet again when they entered their 40s. Again, the

---

[18] American Psychological Association. (n.d.). *Delaying Gratification.* apa.org

individuals who had shown the ability to delay gratification as children and teenagers were likely to enjoy better self-control into middle age.

This research seems to suggest that some people win the genetic lottery when it comes to putting off an instant reward in order to chase a longer-term goal. Brain imaging studies have shown that a **particular part of the brain known as the prefrontal cortex is more active in people with greater self-control.** But there is hope for those of us with a history of impulsive behavior. Another well-established finding in modern psychology is that the brain is plastic.[19] **In simple terms, this means that not only does your neurological wiring affect your behavior, but that you can make changes to your behavior that will then literally shape your brain.** Commit to the habit of delaying gratification and it will become easier over time. Start by making minor changes that enable you to practice the skill of delaying a reward. For example, the next time you want a coffee or soda challenge yourself to wait twenty minutes before going to fetch your drink. **When your phone next buzzes, hold off opening that message for five minutes.** Get used to the idea that sometimes you have to wait for a payoff. Give yourself some praise every time you resist temptation, and over time you'll find that the act of temporarily denying yourself actually becomes pleasant in and of itself. After all, eating that cookie isn't going to make you proud – any idiot can give into temptation and stuff themselves with junk food. Showing some serious self-control, on the other hand, is much harder. Take a moment to appreciate your accomplishment!

Once you have mastered the art of enduring a short wait for a relatively minor reward, take it one step further. Think in terms of days instead of minutes or hours. For example, if you really want to buy a new shirt that you don't need, tell yourself that you can have it if you wait a week. Chances are that by the time the seven days are up, you won't remember why you even wanted the shirt so much in the first place. **When practiced regularly, these exercises will train your mind to excel at delaying gratification.** Even more importantly, you will begin to reconstruct your self-image as someone who can make the right decision and sacrifice what they want in any given moment for what they want in the long term.

Why is this vital to your success? Your self-image is key to achieving your goals and bringing about lasting change. If you believe that you are the kind of person who never plans ahead, makes

---

19 Munte, T.F., Altenmuller, E., & Jancke, L. (2002). The musician's brain as a model of neuroplasticity. *Nature Reviews Neuroscience, 3,* 473-478.

poor decisions and has no control, that is exactly how you will be. **Humans like to act in accordance with their self-image, even if that self-image holds us back.** You already know how affirmations and visualization can shape your self-image and change your behavior. Although the most important step is to practice putting off pleasurable activities on a regular basis, affirmations and visualization will make your efforts even more effective. Repeat "I have great self-control," "I can delay gratification," or another suitable affirmation several times each day. Whenever you decide to delay getting or doing something, **visualize how good it will feel to master temptation and strengthen your self-control even further.**

Stress and fatigue are other factors that directly affect your ability to make smart decisions. Once you understand what psychological research has shown us about impulse control and stress, you can start to plan your day accordingly for much better results. Even those of us with great self-control will have our resolve tested on a frequent basis. **There is a limit as to how much we can handle before our capacity for rational decision-making shuts down.** The trick is to anticipate these limitations in advance and then adjust your routine.

You'll have seen first-hand for yourself that willpower is naturally depleted throughout the afternoon if you've ever gone shopping for dinner after a hectic workday. When you are tired and your mind is churning with stressful thoughts, choosing between a sensible healthy dinner and junk food that offers immediate gratification becomes much harder. **Research has shown that as the day goes on, our willpower weakens.** We can only make so many decisions before our self-control "muscle" becomes fatigued and we start becoming vulnerable to temptation.[20]

Now, let's translate this research into practice. Since your ability to make the right choice in any situation will weaken as the day goes on, it's a good idea to make all your important decisions and start your least pleasant tasks as soon as possible. Save the easy and fun activities for the afternoon and evening to allow for this natural depletion in willpower. It's far easier to choose to work on your boring spreadsheet or report for work rather than browsing Reddit at 9am than it is at 3pm, so when you plan your tasks for the day bear this in mind. As an added bonus, you'll feel proud of yourself for crossing the hardest and most mundane task off your list so early in the day, **which will give you a shot of momentum.** Remember that the Navy SEALs begin each morning by making their beds to a high standard. If this principle is good enough for them, it's

[20] American Psychological Association. (n.d.). *Is Willpower a Limited Resource?* apa.org

good enough for you!

Your blood sugar level also plays a role in your ability to delay gratification. The brain's primary fuel is glucose, and it turns out that when your blood sugar is low it's harder to make smart choices. Research has shown that in both dogs and humans, those with higher blood sugar levels are better at rising above temptation.[21] What does this mean for you? **In order to better resist temptation, try to keep your blood sugar levels steady.** This means eating balanced meals and snacks at regular intervals throughout the day, and not allowing yourself to become too hungry for long periods of time. We all know that hunger often leads to crankiness and an inability to concentrate, so give yourself an advantage by planning a sensible diet. If you are struggling to get or stay productive, take a moment to think about when you last ate a **decent** meal.

In order to meet your goals, you are going to have to make numerous decisions every day – to work on your project or watch TV, to spend money on the latest gadget or invest it in your new business, to work out at the gym or laze around playing games, and so on. Although the choices you make on any given day might seem inconsequential, **over time your ability to resist temptation will make all the difference to how your life turns out.** Take each day seriously as an opportunity to practice the art of restraint and you will become more successful in every area of your life.

---

[21] American Psychological Association. (n.d.). *Is Willpower a Limited Resource?* apa.org

Chapter 17: Why Negative Emotions Can Fuel Your Success

However positive you are and however well you may set yourself up for success, there will be times of despair, sadness, anger, and frustration. To be human is to experience a full spectrum of emotions. Most of us try and shy away from any kind of negative feelings. When we feel bad, we often try to forget about it as soon as possible and get back to feeling happy or at least "OK" as quickly as possible. In this chapter, I'm going to argue that not only is it healthy to embrace your negative emotions, but that they are great fuel when it comes to self-control and bolstering your sense of purpose.

As long as you have come to accept that suffering is inevitable, you are ready to make good use of your unpleasant emotions. **Negative feelings like sadness or despair are clear signals that something is wrong and needs to change.** Think of your negative emotions not as an inconvenience that needs to be "solved," but rather as helpful signposts that highlight what steps you must take in order to improve your quality of life.

Instead of harnessing their negative emotions in a constructive manner, using them as an incentive to put together a plan of action, most people try and ignore uncomfortable feelings. They hope that somehow the problem will resolve itself! We're back again to a central theme of this book – you won't make any solid progress until you back up your thoughts and analysis with concrete action! Let's look at a few specific negative emotions and how you can best channel them. Humans are emotion-driven creatures who gravitate towards drama, so you may as well make the most of your negative energy.

We'll start by taking a fresh look at anger and rage. Lots of us have trouble dealing with these feelings, and much of the trouble comes from how we are socialized. We may have been taught from a young age that it's "not nice" to get angry, and that if we allow ourselves to get angry then we'll spiral out of control. As a result, we suppress even our justifiable rage and seethe with frustration. On the other hand, some of us are taught that anger is a good way to get other people to do what you want. If you live by this rule, you will end up in lots of heated confrontations. Obviously, neither approach is particularly healthy.

Instead, aim to use the physical charge of anger as an energy supply. This could be as simple as channeling your energy into a hard workout at the gym. However, it can also be a great motivator that pushes you towards long term goals. For example, you may be angry at your peers in high school or college for saying or implying that you are fat, stupid, or ugly. You might be able to rise above their comments, but why not use your rage as a basis for positive change? It isn't healthy to base your life decisions on what other people say or do, **but it can certainly propel you forwards.** A desire to prove once and for all that you are not useless, that you can do and be whatever you like and triumph over whatever obstacles life places in your way can give you a much-needed boost when you feel like giving up.

Envy is another powerful negative emotion that you can put to excellent use. When you feel envious, this is a clue that someone else has exactly what you want. This is actually a gift, because it helps you discover precisely what you need to work on. If you catch yourself envying someone else's material possessions, this is a sign that you might want to build up your own wealth. This provides you with a solid starting point for putting together a blueprint for greater financial freedom and security. Look closely at your feelings of envy, write out what it is you want, and during those times when you want to give up return to your list.

What about anxiety? Believe it or not, your tendency to worry can actually work in your favor. Fear can be immobilizing, but used properly it can be the first step towards great success. This can work in two ways. First, conquering your fears is satisfying in and of itself, so imagining how good you will feel when you have done something that scares you is a powerful motivator. Second, you can use fear as a basis for constructive action. For example, let's say that the company you work for is in financial trouble, and your job is at risk. This may be just the push you need to think about applying for a better job, starting your own business, or retraining for a new career. Fear can be managed but rarely obliterated, so you may as well make the most of it!

If you feel overwhelmed by anxiety, sit down and make a list of how you could handle the outcomes you fear most. Assuming that the worst were to happen, how could you make the best of a bad situation? For example, you may be afraid to rent out your house, quit your job and travel the world for a year even though it's one of your most beloved ambitions. Identify what it is that actually frightens you. In this example, you may be afraid that you will be unemployable when you return home. The next step is to think of realistic solutions you could use if your worst fears actually came true. To continue with the above instance, you could retrain for a new career or find an entry-level job in a new sector and spend a couple of years working your way back into better-paying positions. This exercise proves that fear can be a trigger for creative thinking and problem-solving.

Too many people assume that if they are afraid, they are going in the wrong direction. Fear doesn't work like that – in fact, if the thought of making a change or heading in a new direction scares you, it's a positive sign! It means that you are heading out of your comfort zone, which is a necessary condition for progress. Think back to those times in your life when you had to push yourself through a major challenge. You probably felt a strong sense of fear at times, because you were stepping into the unknown. **Never let fear hold you back, and don't fight against it. Accept it as a natural human response, and focus on moving towards your goal step by step.** Everyone feels afraid from time to time. The difference between successful and unsuccessful people is that the former press on anyway and allow their fears to keep them focused on their goals, whereas the latter allow themselves to overthink their situation and become paralyzed.

Despair and sadness are harder to channel into success, but with a bit of imagination they can be a wonderful foundation for self-discipline and achievement. For example, let's say that you have recently gone through a difficult divorce and also lost one of your best friends in the space of a few months. These kinds of events can seriously deplete your focus unless handled properly. A good first step is to remind yourself that everything changes, and that you won't feel like this forever. When we experience a significant loss, it often triggers a period of intense self-reflection. Losses put life into perspective, and suddenly the things that previously seemed so important feel trivial. **When you learn the ability to discern what is actually vital to a good life from what is unnecessary, your focus and time management skills will greatly improve.** The "big things" like following your dreams and pursuing goals suddenly come into focus, and trivial activities such as watching TV or gossiping about other people start to fade into the background. You begin to channel your efforts into achieving something worthwhile rather than merely passing time. Self-discipline becomes easier because you get into the habit of paying attention to what is actually going to help you achieve your aims.

Have you ever read an inspiring story about someone who achieved a big goal in memory of a friend or relative? Some people find that the worst moments in their lives, such as losing a partner to an illness, can prompt them to succeed in ways they could never have imagined. A common example are people who go from being couch potatoes to marathon runners in order to raise money for a relevant charity. These runners often start out with no athletic interests whatsoever, but the knowledge that they are raising money and awareness in someone's memory means that they reorder their priorities. You may also have read about people who become full-time campaigners following horrific events that have taken place in their lives. These examples are proof that negative feelings can be harnessed in a positive manner.

If your goals are creative in nature – for example, you want to write a novel or become a better artist – you'll be encouraged to know that research demonstrates how negativity can help you! Researchers from Ghent University tracked the daily habits and emotions of 102 full-time creative professionals. They discovered that the participants were most productive on days in which they woke up in a bad mood. This suggests that negative feelings can be directly transformed into creative output.[22] Why not immerse yourself in art, music, writing or other similar activity when you next feel angry or sad?

Shame is another unpleasant emotion that holds many of us back from engaging with the world and going after what we want. Note that shame isn't the same as guilt. Guilt is a normal, healthy sensation of having done wrong. Shame, however, is deeper and damages a person's sense of self. When you feel shame, you are in effect telling yourself "I am a bad person." It's hard to put in the work needed to move forward when you have no sense of self-worth. After all, if you think you are fundamentally flawed, you won't feel that you even deserve to make your life better. The good news is that you can deal with shame and develop a healthier attitude.

In her book *Daring Greatly,* author Brene Brown outlines exactly how we can do this. The first step is to open up to someone else about our feelings, because once we gain a sense of acceptance from someone else we are more likely to forgive ourselves. Ask a non-judgmental friend to listen to you as you process guilt and shame, or consider seeing a professional counselor if this is a major problem for you.

There is no need to carry shame around with you – it doesn't help anyone, and it certainly won't help you develop self-discipline. Brown explains that in letting go of shame we grow in compassion, both for ourselves and others. This entails accepting that everyone is human, everyone makes mistakes, and everyone deserves the chance to move on and start again. Remember how we talked about failure earlier on in this book, and established that dwelling on past mistakes drains you of the energy and drive you need to succeed in the present? **Conquering shame is an essential step if you want to de-clutter your mind and focus on what you want most.** Whatever you may have done in the past, you still deserve a positive self-image and the chance of success. Choose to see feelings of shame as a valuable

---

[22] Bledow, R., Rosing, K., & Frese, M. (2013). A Dynamic Perspective on Affect and Creativity. *Academy Of Management Journal, 56, 2,* 432-450.

opportunity to take on a more realistic view of the world and drop the habit of berating yourself.

Chapter 18: Sturgeon's Law & The Pareto Principle

Have you ever become discouraged when your work doesn't turn out as you wanted? In this chapter, you'll learn why it's completely normal to put in hours, days or even years of work and yet feel as though you are going nowhere. More importantly, you'll come to realize why coming to terms with this simple truth is actually very empowering and can help you develop greater self-discipline. We are going to look at two ideas which will change the way you approach your work forever – Sturgeon's Law and the Pareto Principle.

In 1958, science fiction author Theodore Sturgeon wrote an article for *Venture* magazine. He had become increasingly annoyed that critics dismissed science fiction as a low-quality genre, and argued that although it may be true that 90% of science fiction was "crap," the same rule applied to just about everything else! [23] More recently, the philosopher Daniel Dennett identified Sturgeon's Law as one of the seven key tools for critical thinking,[24] proof that it is still influential among academics and writers today.

The Pareto Principle is usually stated in somewhat more positive terms, but the underlying theme is the same. In 1896, Italian economist Vilfredo Pareto published a paper in which he showed that 20% of the Italian people owned 80% of all the land in Italy, and that just 20% of the pea pods growing in his garden yielded 80% of the peas he harvested. In the 20th century, this observation became known as "the 80/20 rule," or "the law of the vital few."[25] The Pareto Principle has become the basis for a number of business guidelines or rules of thumb. The best-known may be the old adage that states "80% of your business comes from 20% of your customers."

Having learned about Sturgeon's Law, you may be starting to wonder why anyone should bother putting in lots of time and effort on a project if it's likely to be rubbish. If whatever you produce stands a 90% chance of being crap, why start at all? The Pareto Principle tells us that only 20%

---

[23] Wikipedia. (2017). *Sturgeon's law.* wikipedia.org
[24] Jones, J. (2013). *Daniel Dennett Presents Seven Tools For Critical Thinking.* openculture.com
[25] Wikipedia. (2017). *Pareto principle.* wikipedia.org

of our efforts are going to yield any significant results, which is slightly more encouraging but is still a little off-putting.

Yet these theories teach us several valuable lessons, which underline the value of developing self-discipline. First, they encourage us to realize that it is completely normal to work hard and yet be unable to predict what will pay off and what won't. For example, say that you are an author and are writing a series of books. Over the course of a couple of years you release four novels. Three only sell a few copies, but one is a smash hit and wins you lots of fans. If you hadn't heard of the Pareto Principle, you might be surprised and disappointed that only a quarter of your published works were successful. You might be discouraged from writing anything else, convinced that you just aren't talented enough. On the other hand, if you understood the 80/20 rule your perspective would be entirely different. You would be congratulating yourself on your success and probably feel inspired to write even more books! Keeping your expectations realistic means that isolated triumphs and disasters don't blow you off course. **It helps you keep a broader perspective, which is crucial in maintaining the day-to-day momentum and self-discipline you need to stay on track.**

Once you accept that only a relatively small proportion of your work will make a difference, you have an incentive to work as hard and as smart as possible. You also have an excellent reason to try as many different approaches as you can if the first, second or third doesn't work. Successful CEOs are familiar with this concept. That's why they are willing to take risks on new products and services whilst never giving up when the majority fail. They know full well that no-one can be successful most of the time, and that the best way to insulate yourself against disappointment is to anticipate difficulties.

The 80/20 rule can also be exciting when you think about it in the right way. Whilst 80% of your work might not land you the results you want, the remaining fifth will propel you forwards towards success. This creates a degree of uncertainty – which projects will flounder, and which will flourish? Although you might wish that you could predict the future, most of us thrive on ambiguity to some extent. Your very best work could be just around the corner. If you don't stick to your goals and plans, you'll never know what could have been. Isn't that a powerful thought? **Despite the fact that even top performers fail on a regular basis, they only need one or two major successes to be considered brilliant. This also applies to you.** It really doesn't matter if some of your ideas are lousy, provided you have the self-discipline to just keep going.

Even if what you produce is absolute garbage, taking a positive attitude towards the end result will set you up for eventual success. Just because a project fails or hasn't turned out quite as you would like doesn't mean that you cannot learn from it! When something goes wrong, muster the courage to examine why it didn't work out. Don't dwell on failure, but always extract the lessons it can teach you. If nothing else, a failed project will have provided you with a chance to practice the art of self-discipline. When you spend several hours each day on a project, you have at least proven to yourself that you have the ability to focus your attention and overcome procrastination, and that is valuable in itself.

When you figure out what does work, build on it for repeated success. This may sound obvious – doesn't everyone know that when something works, the smartest thing to do is replicate it? Unfortunately, this isn't always easy. It requires self-discipline to take a step back and assess what is moving you towards your goals and what isn't. **The difficulty comes when what you want to work and what actually does work don't quite align.** For example, suppose you found a company that creates and sells video games. You and your fellow founder personally enjoy classic arcade-style games and release three in the first twelve months. At the same time, you have also carried out market research that suggests a car-themed racing game would also sell well, so despite the fact that neither of you particularly enjoy playing or creating games in this genre you also release a racing game. The sales figures are clear – the gaming public much prefer to race onscreen cars than play modern versions of arcade classics.

What would you do next? The sensible option would be to further research what it is that people like so much about racing games and then build on your success by releasing another such game. If you kept the 80/20 rule in mind, you wouldn't be surprised to learn that most of your sales came from only one of your games. However, if you personally have an emotional tie to arcade games then you might be tempted to build yet another product in this category. Your hope that the next arcade game will be a success overrides your more sensible side that takes notice of the sales figures. **Taking an honest look at what is working and what isn't requires self-discipline and the ability to put your emotional investment to one side.**

If you've ever wondered why this is so difficult to do, know that you are not alone. Humans tend to continue investing in projects or ideas that we have already started or feel an attachment to, whether or not it's to our own benefit. On occasion, this attachment to a certain outcome can be healthy. The more determined you are to lose weight, the greater the chance that you'll endure a difficult diet and grueling exercise regimen. **People who lose serious amounts of weight**

through strict diets often gain enough momentum through their commitment and ensuing results that they make a substantial effort to keep the weight off.

Unfortunately, we also tend to stick with projects that are going nowhere fast even when they are hurting our bank balance or psychological wellbeing. In layman's terms, this is known as "throwing good money after bad." Psychologists call it the "sunk cost fallacy."[26] It might seem ridiculous to onlookers, but when you are invested in a particular outcome it's hard to admit that you have made the wrong decision. Most of us are proud, and to walk away from a failing project can be painful. Yet if you accept that most of your efforts are unlikely to give you the results you want, you will be able to acquire the skill of knowing when to give up gracefully. This doesn't mean celebrating failure, **but rather having the wisdom to realize that it benefits you in the long run to sacrifice a fantasy in order to build on what you actually have.**

As a general rule, training yourself to remain focused on what is going on in the present is a far healthier and more productive way to live than acting on "could bes" and "maybes." In the next chapter you'll learn how to implement an Eastern approach to therapy that teaches us to accept reality as it is whilst taking steps to change our lives.

---

[26] Leahy, R.L. (2014). *Letting Go of Sunk Costs.* psychologytoday.com

Chapter 19: Morita Therapy

If you've ever been to therapy, you'll know that the Western school of counseling goes something like this: You and your therapist work together to identify your problems, then your therapist tries to help you conquer them by adjusting your behavior, thoughts, or both. In this chapter, I'm going to outline a different way of working with fear and procrastination that will help you get over mental barriers and sharpen your self-discipline. You will learn about a set of Japanese techniques known as "Morita therapy." This approach has helped thousands of people to lead calmer, more productive lives.

According to the To Do Institute, Morita therapy was founded by a Japanese psychiatrist called Shoma Morita approximately a hundred years ago.[27] At first, he was attempting to develop a treatment for anxiety inspired by the teachings of Zen Buddhism. However, his basic ideas gradually spread and are now applied to various psychological problems both in Japan and other countries.

Morita built his therapy on the principle of "arugamama," a Japanese term which in English roughly translates to "the acceptance of the world as it is." **Morita believed that we don't necessarily have to try and change or process our emotions in order to lead fulfilling and contented lives.** In fact, he emphasized that the best approach was to notice our feelings, accept them, **but then move to addressing the steps we then have to take in order to reach a goal.** Attempting to force our feelings into something new can compound the issue, because when it doesn't work we become frustrated and disheartened. We become locked in a destructive cycle whereby **we notice negative emotions, dwell on them, stop taking any action, perceive ourselves as failures for not achieving anything, experience more negative emotions, and so on.**

Morita also put forward a two-part theory of human nature, saying that everyone is driven by two distinct desires. The first desire is to reach our full potential as human beings, a process known as "self-actualization." This drive is what pushes us to go after our goals and try to be a better person. This underpins self-discipline, especially when we can tap into this desire on a regular basis. Fulfilling our potential, or the idea of chasing achievement, is extremely rewarding. However, we also have another drive that pushes us to remain in one place – a longing for

---

[27] To Do Institute. (n.d.). *Morita Therapy.* todoinstitute.org

stability and comfort.[28] This is why we often feel reluctant to chase any dream that could result in failure, even if intellectually we know that achieving it will bring us closer to the person we want to be.

Thoughts can be the enemy of action. Of course you need to think deeply from time to time, but it's possible to overdo it! As you probably know from experience, when you begin to worry about your worries or subject your fear to in-depth analysis, you don't often feel better. In fact, you tend to feel worse. Our inner states are difficult to explain away, and you can drive yourself mad if you try. **The more you focus on your negative emotions and overthink them, the stronger they become. It all comes back to making a choice about where you direct your attention.** When you choose to think about your current struggles, you are setting yourself up for further anxiety and resistance. On the other hand, Morita therapists believe that once you tune into the underlying desires that actually underpin your anxieties, you can then move onto making practical progress.

For example, someone who experiences a lot of anxiety in social situations would be encouraged not to think about the symptoms of panic they feel when interacting with other people, but to instead focus on their desire for better relationships with friends and family. They would then be helped to put together a practical plan for meeting their needs, such as planning outings or practicing conversation skills. Morita therapists do not deny that their clients suffer, but they teach them how to simply "let it be" rather than analyzing the past or encouraging them to dwell on negative experiences.

Those who practice Morita therapy believe that the Western approach to mental health and illness encourages people to concentrate too much on labels and not enough on constructive living. If you are suffering with a mental or emotional problem and consult a doctor trained in conventional Western medicine, they are likely to give you a label such as "depressed," "suffering from OCD," "suffering from social anxiety," and so forth. From that point on, the person who has received this label begins to think of themselves in these terms rather than as a powerful individual who can choose to improve their own life. The stigma attached to mental health problems makes things even worse, because the patient not only has to deal with the negative thoughts and behaviors that lead them to seek help in the first place, but they also begin to obsess over what others think of them.

---

[28] Morita School. (n.d.). *Morita Therapy.* moritaschool.com

Traditional Morita treatment consists of four stages.[29] The first consists of complete rest, in order to help the patient arrive at a state of calm. No stimulating materials such as television are permitted. This break from the usual stresses of day-to-day life enables the patient to become self-aware again and ready to pay attention to what is really important in their lives. After a week of rest, the patient is usually bored and excited to get involved in activities again with even the most mundane of tasks now having fresh appeal. They are now ready for the second and third stages – light activity followed by moderate physical work.

Initially they will be asked to take walks outside, reconnecting with the natural world and learning how to live in the present. Does this sound familiar? Remember, Morita was heavily influenced by Zen Buddhism, which teaches that living in the here and now is the most sensible approach to life. After a couple of days the patient will then begin to carry out simple practical tasks such as gardening or cleaning. The idea is that in doing practical work, **the patient will learn to switch their focus away from their innermost thoughts and onto the outside world**.

Although traditional Morita therapy takes place in a residential setting, you don't have to go anywhere to apply its lessons to your own life. The main takeaway is that action, rather than analysis, is incredibly healing. It may not take away all your self-doubts, sadness and other negative emotions, but it certainly helps you find a sense of meaning. Accept that you may not always want to work or put in the effort needed to meet your goals. It's perfectly normal. **It doesn't actually matter how you feel when you get up in the morning. All that actually counts is what you do.** This is the very heart of self-discipline - the act of keeping going even when you would rather give up or switch to an easier task. There is no need to feel ashamed of your feelings. The key is to accept them, and just carry on. **When you achieve your goal, what's going to matter? How you felt on a day-to-day basis, or the fact that you made it in the end?** Chances are that you won't even remember how your mood fluctuated as you took steps towards your goal, but you will certainly remember whether or not you achieved the end result!

As you probably don't have access to a Morita therapist, some self-talk is a useful tool when you need to implement the principles. When you catch yourself resisting work, perhaps because you

---

[29] Ishiyama, I. (2003). A Bending Willow Tree: A Japanese (Morita Therapy) Model of Human Nature and Client Change. *Canadian Journal of Counselling, 37, 3,* 216-231.

feel as though you are bound to fail or perhaps because you are obsessively thinking over past memories, take a minute to address yourself out loud. I do this when I hit a slump, and it really works! For example, I recently felt completely unmotivated to write a report up for a client. Remembering what I had learned in my studies of Morita therapy, I sat at my desk and channeled my inner therapist. "Look," I said to myself, "You don't feel like working right now. You feel a bit low. That's fine. You can't control that. But what you can control is whether you keep going, so do that. Keep on writing." Talking to yourself may sound a bit strange, but it can make a huge difference. If you work with other people and can't talk to yourself out loud without risking stares or strange comments, use your inner voice or write some useful phrases on small sticky notes.

Once you fully understand the Morita framework, you'll appreciate that we don't have to wait until we feel confident before we take a risk, or be free of anxiety before we do something that scares us. Our feelings fluctuate depending on internal and external circumstances, and at times there is little we can do to control them. Your feelings will no longer be an excuse for why you aren't acting. This can be a scary thought, so work on shifting your perspective slowly. Think of a small task that makes you feel scared, bored or unhappy in another way. For example, you may know that your closet needs a good clean but the idea makes you feel bored. You know that it won't be an enjoyable job. Tasks like this are actually a perfect way to embrace Morita principles. In this example, you could tell yourself that whilst the job will be boring, you will do it anyway. As you begin the physical work of sorting through your clothes and shoes, you will find that your internal monologue begins to quieten. **If you allow yourself to become fully immersed in the job at hand, you may discover that practical work is soothing when carried out with a mindful attitude.**

Accepting your feelings is an alien concept to most of us raised in a Western culture. We have been taught that problem-solving is a valuable skill, and that we can apply logical reasoning to our emotions. It's true that reason is a great tool, but we over-value it in some cases. Think back to those times in your life when you experienced a very strong emotion. Could you have reasoned your way out of it? Probably not. For example, if you experience the breakup of a romantic relationship or the death of a parent, there is not much you can do with those emotions other than let them "just be" and fade away. **Ironically, the less you fight against them the quicker they will leave you in peace!**

Morita therapy also teaches us that our feelings don't have to determine the outcome. Yes, your mindset is important – positive thinking will generally yield better results over the long-term.

However, the Morita framework proves that even when you are sad or depressed, you can still take constructive action. You can get up in the morning feeling blue but choose to sit with your feelings and get on with your day regardless. Chances are that most of the work you do will be no better or worse, but you will feel better by the end of the day. **What's more, your positive emotions and confidence level will snowball with each productive week as you reap the fruits of your labor.**

Also, do you remember the study I mentioned in the previous chapter on channeling your negative emotions? Creative people are often most productive when their days begin on a low note! If they can accept their negative feelings, work alongside them and even make them into something wonderful, then so can you.

Although it is action-oriented, Morita therapy demonstrates that proper rest is important. Sometimes we need to take a break from our hectic lives before we go mad! There is no virtue in working yourself to the point of burnout and fatigue. In the next chapter, we'll take a closer look at the signs of burnout and how you can prevent it derailing your self-discipline.

Chapter 20: Avoiding Burnout

So far, this book has focused on how you can remain disciplined even in the face of obstacles and circumstances that deplete your willpower. However, you also need to remember that you can push yourself too far, sometimes with devastating consequences. In this chapter, I'm going to teach you everything you need to know about the curse of those who enjoy high levels of self-discipline - burnout. You'll learn how to spot the signs, how to recover quickly, and why people can end up emotionally and physically destroyed by their responsibilities. The good news is that even the most stressed and burnt out people can bounce back, but prevention is always better than cure.

Let's clarify what burnout really is. It's normal to feel stressed from time to time or even on a daily basis if you're going through a tough period at work or home. When things feel too overwhelming, it seems as though your capacity for action and even rational thought shuts down. Most of us have experienced this kind of "brain freeze" at some point. Usually it lasts for a few minutes, perhaps a couple of hours. Taking a brief break from work or approaching the situation from a different angle is often enough to put us back on course. This temporary state is a protective mechanism. It helps us regain self-control and decreases anxiety levels.

However, when someone burns out this kind of recovery is impossible. A burnt out person has reached breaking point. **They can no longer physically or mentally cope with all the demands life is throwing their way.** In extreme cases, they may have to seek psychiatric help and take an extended leave of absence from work. Burnout is both a physical and mental state that encompasses exhaustion, low mood, feelings of hopelessness, and a lack of ability to make decisions.[30] The stereotypical image of burnout in popular culture is the executive who takes on far too much work, putting in 16-hour days until they "snap" or "go mad." However, you can suffer burnout as a full-time parent or part-time employee – it all depends on your coping skills, personality, and how much pressure you place on yourself.

To make matters worse, someone suffering burnout often interprets it as a reflection on their capabilities or worth as a person. They may see others around them who appear to be coping just fine, and wonder what it is that they lack. The irony is that it tends to be high achievers with great self-discipline who are the most prone to burnout in the first place. When you are unafraid

---

[30] Carter, D. (2013). *The Tell Tale Signs of Burnout..Do You Have Them?* psychologytoday.com

to take on demanding roles and push yourself to the limit, you may be tempted to skimp on rest and relaxation. In the short term this can be a reasonable strategy. For example, if you are in the closing stages of a large-scale business deal, it won't do you much harm to put in a few late nights. It's when work-life imbalance becomes a normal way of life that problems arise. As you develop your self-discipline, you need to be careful not to stretch yourself too far. Fortunately, burnout doesn't happen randomly or suddenly. No-one feels fine on a Monday then becomes burnt out on Tuesday. This means that as long as you keep an eye on how you are feeling, burnout is entirely preventable.

Odd as it may sound, in order to stop burnout you need to harness your self-discipline, albeit in a different direction! The trick is that along with the ability to get things done, you also need to develop the knack of saying "no" to tasks and projects that will leave you drained whilst sticking to a healthy routine. It's absolutely essential that you sleep at least six hours per night, drink enough water throughout the day to remain hydrated, and eat well-balanced meals. This might not sound very exciting when you are in the middle of an all-consuming project, but you won't be able to make good decisions and perform to a high level if you are tired and malnourished. Remember that your willpower is depleted when you are fatigued, so regular sleep and meals that provide you with a steady stream of energy will raise your chances of success.

Commit to making time for relaxation and fun! If you bombard yourself with endless tasks and difficult decisions all day every day, it's inevitable that you will burn out. Having some downtime isn't just fun and good for morale, it's also necessary for ensuring optimum performance. Even Shaolin monks and members of the Special Forces aren't expected to train or work all day every day. They know that too much mental and physical pressure is detrimental to their determination and self-control.

When you do make time to relax, ensure that you do it properly. Don't keep checking your phone for notifications, and don't allow yourself to worry about your latest work project. Apply the principles of Morita therapy and give yourself a break from the stress of the outside world when you start to feel overwhelmed.

Keeping your troubles in perspective will stop you attaching too much meaning to your thoughts, and in turn keep your anxiety levels manageable. When you are in the middle of a major project or stressing yourself out over problems in your personal life, it's easy to forget that in the grand scheme of things your issues are pretty insignificant. Of course, you want to do your best and strive for success, but even if you fail it isn't the end of the world. You can try again, and failure needn't define you.

Often it isn't the workload itself that drives people to burnout – it's how they choose to think about it. Again, it all comes down to choice in how you frame your experiences. You can choose to view your work as a burden that will inevitably cause you a lot of stress. Alternatively, you can apply what you have learned about positive thinking and decide that although a project might demand a lot of effort from you at the moment, in the long run it will pay dividends.

You can also use your self-discipline to help you manage your workload, which will lower your stress levels and help you spot potential problems before they start. **If you give in to procrastination and trivial distractions, the important stuff will pile up.** You will then be forced to put in more hours than you would like over a shorter period of time, which may result in burnout that needn't have happened in the first place! When you are excited and motivated at the start of a project, you may fall into the trap of thinking that everything will somehow fit together and get done. This is a mistake. **Even the most competent, brilliant people need a framework of some kind to perform at a high level.**

The most effective practical solution to this common problem is scheduling. Take action immediately at the beginning of a project by establishing the exact steps you need to take along with a realistic estimate of how much time you will need to put in. If you aren't sure, ask someone more knowledgeable and experienced for help. If in doubt, assume that tasks will take roughly one and a half times as long as you originally thought. This is a win-win approach – if you finish early, you can use the extra time to relax or get a head start on the next step. If you take longer than you originally planned, you can feel safe in the knowledge that you accounted for this eventuality at the beginning.

I find this kind of scheduling particularly helpful when it comes to writing up various kinds of reports and compiling presentations. When I first began working as a freelance consultant, I had to guess roughly how long it would take me to produce a document. Working blind like this forced me to work late nights to get a project done or alternatively leave me with gaps in my schedule when I finished early! Over time, I've learned that keeping a simple spreadsheet of tasks together with the time it usually takes is really helpful in planning my upcoming week. Sometimes I wish I'd asked other people working in my field how long I should allow for certain tasks, but then again there's no substitute for learning the hard way through personal experience. You'd think that planning out upcoming work is an obvious strategy, but people often fail to sit down and do it. Why? Usually, the answer can be explained in one word – fear. Scheduling means looking closely at a project and allowing the reality of the situation to really sink in – you are going to have to work hard, there are going to be challenges, and there's always the chance that it won't go to plan. The only solution is to acknowledge these feelings, sit with them, and take action regardless. You will never wake up one morning and suddenly feel confident about that tricky assignment you've been delaying. In fact, your anxiety will only worsen until you suck it up, set aside ten minutes and commit your thoughts to paper (or screen). Appreciate this early on in your career and you'll be more productive and less stressed than the majority of your co-workers.

As you can see, there are plenty of practical tips and techniques you can use for preventing burnout. But what if you are already there, feeling utterly exhausted and sick at the thought of yet another day at work? **Like it or not, you are going to have to take some time to give your mind and body some rest.** If someone told you that they had suffered a heart attack or broken their arm, you wouldn't judge them for taking some time off. **The same logic applies to victims of burnout, including you.**

Just one week can be enough to restore your mental balance, but you need to be upfront with your employer (if you have one), clients (if you are a freelancer) and doctor. It's your responsibility to seek the help you need. Fortunately, employers are increasingly concerned about work-life balance and many will understand if you are suffering signs of burnout. Depending on who is most approachable, talk with your manager or a member of staff from HR. They may ask you to provide a doctor's note depending how severe your symptoms are and how much sick leave you will require. This is standard procedure, and doesn't mean that they don't believe you.

As you recover from burnout, take some time to reflect on what you could learn from the experience. Burnout does not mean you are failure or cannot cope with your job. **However, it's a sure sign that the way you approach your work needs to change.** Just as with any other lifestyle shift, self-discipline and a willingness to learn from what has gone wrong will help you make constructive changes. **Think back on the signs that you were heading for burnout, and come up with a list of strategies that could prevent it happening again.** For example, if your burnout was triggered when your colleague went on maternity leave and you volunteered to take over her workload, you need to think carefully about how you schedule tasks in the future. Striking the balance between pushing yourself to the limit and safeguarding your mental health is a skill, and sometimes it requires taking a few knocks along the way.

Chapter 21: Why You Resist Change – The Status Quo Bias

Now that you are nearing the end of this book, you will have learned almost everything you need to know in order to boost your self-discipline and harness it to achieve your goals. However, from time to time you may still run up against a mental block. You might know precisely what you want to achieve, have mastered the art of taking action even when you don't feel like it, and conquered your fear of failure. Yet some invisible force might be holding you back. This can be very frustrating, but it's quite common to feel this way. In this chapter, you'll learn about a psychological phenomenon known as the "status quo bias" and how it can undermine even the most determined and self-disciplined of individuals. Fortunately, once you are aware of how it operates you can strike back and regain the self-discipline needed to reach your goals.

Psychologists have always been interested in self-defeating behaviors. One of the most famous examples is the sunk cost fallacy. The status quo bias is less well-known but still essential knowledge for anyone interested in self-development. **It explains why we tend to remain stuck in a particular situation even when we tell everyone else (and ourselves!) that we'd rather have or be something else.** You will have experienced this for yourself if you have stayed around in a relationship that was well past its natural expiration date, or remained in a boring job even though you had the chance to go after a new position.

Simply put, the status quo bias describes the human tendency to prefer what they already have or what is familiar rather than pursue the unknown. Just like the Pareto Principle, it has its roots in economics rather than psychology. Back in 1988, economists William Samuelson and Richard Zeckhauser published a series of studies in the *Journal of Risk and Uncertainty*. They pointed out that although economic theory tries to predict how people will choose between two or more alternatives, in the real world people often elect to do nothing and carry on as before.[31]

So why is it that so many of us stick with the same old people, jobs, and even ambitions? Several

---

[31] Samuelson, W., & Zeckhauser, R. (1988). Status Quo Bias in Decision Making. *Journal of Risk and Uncertainty, 1,* 7-59.

reasons have been put forward to explain this phenomenon.[32] First, consider loss aversion theory. Humans are very sensitive to any possibility that they may lose something, even if that "something" (such as a mediocre job or lousy relationship) really wasn't that great in the first place. **It often takes a lot of evidence that an alternative is actually going to improve our lives before we make a leap of faith.** Despite the fact that making a change often leads to a more positive outcome, people tend to assume on a subconscious level that any form of change is "bad" and threatening. Change – even when it's positive, such as the change that comes with getting married or moving to a nicer home – requires effort and thought. This represents a very real cost, and sometimes we don't feel like paying it.

Another factor behind the status quo bias is a fear of regret. No-one likes to feel as though they have made a poor choice, because typically they believe it reflects badly on them as an individual. They may also worry that other people will judge them for being stupid or ignorant. Therefore, they default to simply sticking with what they already know. They may worry that if they take a risk and actually make changes, it'll backfire in some way and they won't be any better off. The reality is that failure is never final. You can always try a new angle or set yourself a new, more attainable goal. Sometimes we believe that if we make a mistake, we can't be trusted to try new things ever again.

The mere exposure effect is another powerful mind trick that can keep you locked into the same old beliefs, behaviors and routines. Research spanning several decades has demonstrated that the more we encounter a particular phenomenon, the more likely we are to accept and like it. For example, a classic study from the 1960s showed that the more often participants were exposed to words and symbols, the more likely they were to develop a positive attitude towards them.[33] You may have noticed that the more you interact with a particular person, the more you grow to like them. Of course, there are exceptions to this rule, but **in general the more time we spend in a situation the more we tend to assume that even if it isn't exactly what we want, it's at least "OK" or "good enough."**

The mere exposure effect can work both for and against you. If you are working towards developing better habits and leading a life of self-discipline, here's the good news: **When self-**

---

[32] Anderson, C.J. (2003). The psychology of doing nothing: Forms of decision avoidance result from reason and emotion. *Psychological Bulletin, 129, 1,* 139-167.

[33] Zajonc, R.B. (1968). Attitudinal Effects of Mere Exposure. *Journal of Personality and Social Psychology Monograph Supplement, 9, 2,* 1-27.

control becomes your new normal, you'll be less likely to revert back to your old ways. The more time you spend in a positive frame of mind, the more likely it is that an upbeat approach to life will seem "right" and comfortable. On the other hand, your natural human tendency towards sticking with the status quo and favoring your old habits means that making changes can be challenging. You may not want to laze around in bed all morning on a Saturday, but if it's what you've done for years then you'll have to fight hard against your status quo bias! Remind yourself that the more often you get up early, the easier it will become.

Now that you understand how and why the status quo bias is so common, think about those times in your past when you have been faced with a tough decision or the chance to change your life. On reflection, do you think that this maladaptive kind of thinking could have played a role? Perhaps you found yourself saying things like "Well, that's the way I've always done it," or "If it ain't broke, don't fix it!" **The status quo bias might keep you safe, but it will also keep you trapped in the same situation.** It can also breed regret in the long term. One of the worst feelings in the world arises when you look back over your life and regret the chances you never took. Fortunately, a little self-awareness will help you make better choices in the future.

From now on, you are going to draw upon your rational decision-making abilities to help you shape the life you want. **Whenever you face a choice between sticking with what you currently have and pursuing a new situation or goal, challenge yourself to complete the following exercise.**

You need to draw up a four-part list that will force you to see your own thoughts laid out in a logical manner. Divide a page into quarters. Use them to write out the following: Advantages of the status quo, Disadvantages of the status quo, Advantages to the alternative under consideration, and Disadvantages to the alternative under consideration. **Give yourself at least ten minutes to complete your lists.** Let yourself sleep on what you have written, then return to them the following day. Ask a trusted friend or relative to help you if you worry that you'll overlook something, or if you just want a second opinion. **Do bear in mind that everyone falls victim to the status quo bias from time to time, so be discerning when taking advice from others.**

Remember that your feelings should not have the final say in your decisions. You now know that negative feelings are not a problem – you can live with them and take action anyway. You can also channel the positive energy that moves you closer towards your goals. Or, of course, you can do both! **It's normal to feel anxiety at the thought of making even constructive**

changes that will benefit you in the long run. Remind yourself that you can choose to acknowledge doubts and then act as though you are unafraid. Taking action will show you that there is often little to fear anyway, and **much of your worries are usually the result over-thinking and pessimism.** Yes, everything could go wrong – **but then again, everything could go right!**

In some instances, it doesn't matter whether you fall back on the status quo bias. If you are choosing a sandwich for lunch, whether you stick with your usual cheese filling or try the chicken mayonnaise probably won't alter the course of your life. However, revisiting these small decisions is a good way to practice taking a more rational approach to making choices. **Get into the habit of questioning those parts of your day-to-day routine that usually go unexamined.** You will learn the art of actively noticing your habits – both good and bad – and pursuing alternatives.

It may shock you to realize that you have been doing the same things over and over again for months or even years. In all likelihood, you drink the same kind of coffee or tea every morning, buy the same brand of toothpaste every time you go to the store, and go to the same restaurants whenever you go out to eat. Don't feel bad – most of us fall into a rut because we don't even consider challenging the status quo! **Yet if you want to take charge of your life, you must be more proactive in monitoring your habits and taking care not to fall into the same old routine.** Begin on a small scale by challenging yourself to listen to a new radio station, trying a new place to eat, or buying a piece of clothing that isn't your usual style. Be willing to embrace the possibility that **mixing things up is the best (and perhaps only) way of making progress.** Once you prove to yourself that change can be good, this will start to shape how you approach more important issues such as making a career change, leaving an unhealthy relationship, or overhauling your diet.

Our habits and embedded preferences keep us locked in the same old routines, day in and day out. **You can now appreciate why trying to change one area of your life in isolation seldom works.** For example, if you want to get into the habit of going to the gym three nights a week after work, this is unlikely to be successful if you stick with your usual routine of only getting six hours of sleep, eating junk food, and working too hard at the office. **It's better to aim for a more thoughtful, self-aware and self-disciplined approach to life in general rather than forcing change in one area.**

When you recognize and eliminate your status quo bias, self-discipline and commitment to your goals will seem easier. If you favor what is familiar and "safe," you will find it hard to start a new routine that could change your life in any significant way. Remaining open to new ways of living leaves you free to focus on what you want rather than fixating on safeguarding what you already have. **It makes you less afraid of failure and instead fills you with a sense of excitement at what lies ahead.** It's then up to you to take action and go after what you really want!

Chapter 22: The Dunning-Kruger Effect

When you start learning how to control yourself around temptation and build on your capacity for self-discipline, you'll begin to feel better about yourself. This is only natural, because being able to focus your attention and smash your goals is incredibly rewarding. You definitely deserve to be congratulated, so don't be afraid to give yourself some praise and a few rewards from time to time. However, this book ends on a cautionary note. As you become more confident in your ability to control yourself and lead a disciplined life, it's wise to remain realistic when assessing your own competence. In this chapter, you'll learn about what can happen when people lose the ability to accurately assess their competence, and how you can guard against it.

Everyone has at least one friend, relative or colleague who is out of touch with reality when it comes to appraising their own skills. For example, most of us have a family member who describes themselves as having "a great sense of humor" yet tells only terrible jokes. You may have a more realistic grasp on your own aptitude, but it's useful to remember that in general people tend to overestimate their competence across a variety of domains.

The Dunning-Kruger Effect refers to an instance whereby an individual is not only incompetent in one or more areas, but also fails to realize just how limited their ability really is. Someone suffering from this problem therefore has what is known as a "double burden." They will keep making mistakes in the same area over and over again, and will also struggle to correct them because they lack insight into their own deficiencies.[34] Rather than

---

[34] Dunning, D. (2011). The Dunning-Kruger Effect: On Being Ignorant of One's Own Ignorance. *Advances in Experimental Social Psychology, 44,* 247.

look to improve their skills, those afflicted will sincerely believe that they are more than capable and any negative outcomes are the result of bad luck.

Justin Kruger and David Dunning, two psychologists based at Cornell University, have found that this phenomenon shows up when you test people on their grammatical knowledge, logic skills, and humor. It turns out that those objectively measured as being the worst at these skills (i.e. they score in the bottom 25% of their demographic) are the least likely to judge their performance with any degree of accuracy.[35] This is because they have weak or non-existent metacognition, metamemory, and metacomprehension. They don't seem to be able to think properly about their own thinking processes, or take a critical view of their own understanding. **In short, they lack the the ability to monitor their own performance.**

Kruger and Dunning use the example of grammar. To write a well-structured sentence you need to remember how to implement the rules of grammar, how to rectify any mistakes, and how to tell the difference between grammatically correct and incorrect sentences. You need sound underlying knowledge if you are to pass accurate judgment on any given sentence – the very same knowledge that you need in order to establish whether your own opinion is right! Before this theory became widely known, psychologists had already established that most people think they are better than average on many dimensions, including leadership potential and written expression.[36] The Dunning-Kruger effect is just an extreme version of this common human tendency. It can have significant implications in a range of settings. For instance, you may have come across members of senior management teams who appear completely incompetent yet have secured numerous promotions. If you remember that incompetent people are blissfully unaware of their ignorance and shortcomings whereas the more able are relatively modest, suddenly this phenomenon doesn't seem quite so mysterious.

So how does this relate to self-discipline? If you think of self-discipline and self-control as skills – and they are indeed skills, just like playing an instrument - you will realize that it's possible to overestimate your ability in these areas. If you catch yourself thinking that you have truly mastered the art of resisting temptation and remaining productive at all times, watch out! You may be right, but on the other hand, you might be completely unaware that you have a long

---

[35] Kruger, J., & Dunning, D. (1999). Unskilled and Unaware of It: How Difficulties in Recognizing One's Own Incompetence Lead to Inflated Self-Assessments. *Journal of Personality and Social Psychology, 77, 6*, 1121-1134.
[36] Ibid, p.1122.

way to go in this area.

This research implies that the more you know about a subject or the more proficient you become in a particular skill, the less willing you are to label yourself an "expert." It's a kind of paradox – the more you know, the more you appreciate that there is still a lot more to learn! **It's about striking a balance between maintaining a positive self-image as a competent person whilst at the same time being willing to take on board objective feedback.** This will ensure that you never slip into complacency and become one of those smug, annoying people who aren't even aware of their own deficiencies.

What do I mean by "objective feedback"? It can take the form of number-based goals such as money earned or projects completed. It can also take the form of unbiased assessment of your efforts by strangers. For example, let's say you think that you are a good driver. As a result, you apply to take an advanced driving test in order to gain a driving qualification that reduces your insurance premium or gives you the chance to get a driving-based job. During the test, the driving instructor tells you in no uncertain terms that you have a way to go before you will reach the standard they are looking for.

This kind of reality check can be harsh, but we all need someone or something to bring us back down to earth. It can prompt us to think about where we are going, and how we can improve.

Along with objective feedback, the best defence against the Dunning-Kruger effect is to pursue self-development and always strive for improvement. The better you are at something, the better your ability to judge your own competence. Therefore, you need to take every opportunity to hone and practice your skills whenever possible. Dunning and Kruger discovered that when they trained research participants in the art of solving logic problems, they not only solved more problems but also gained insight into how their performance ranked in comparison to others. This finding doesn't just apply to laboratory tasks, but is also relevant to everyday skills and the pursuit of goals. **As far as self-discipline is concerned, it's a case of implementing the techniques outlined in this book – learning how to continue working even when you don't feel like it, channeling your negative feelings, thinking positively, and so on – on a regular basis.** Your self-awareness will grow along with your competence. The most self-disciplined people will never tell you that they don't get distracted or never have a bad day. Having worked hard to become focused and productive, they appreciate how far they have come whilst never losing sight of the potential for further improvement.

Adopt a "keep on learning" policy. Whether you want to learn a martial art, further your career or take up a new hobby, never assume that you've learned or seen it all. Thanks to the internet it's never been easier to access all the information and tutorials you could ever need. Why not start an online course or download an app designed to help you improve your knowledge or skills in only a few minutes a day? Many are free and also provide you with objective feedback. For example, language-learning apps often keep a log of your test scores. **This will prevent you from becoming overconfident whilst also allowing you to celebrate your progress over time.**

Along with keeping a record of concrete goals and results, you can guard yourself against the Dunning-Kruger Effect **by engaging with other people who are already where you want to be, and calibrating your skills against theirs.** Note that this doesn't give you licence to start comparing yourself and then being disappointed when you fall short of your idols. However, keeping an eye on the distance between where you currently are and where you want to end up will keep you rooted in reality. If you can talk or write to someone you consider a leader or aspirational figure, ask them whether they consider themselves an expert in what they do. Chances are that they'll tell you in no uncertain terms that there's still a lot left for them to learn! The most inspirational leaders are often the most humble. Not only do they admit that their knowledge is limited, but they will also be the first to talk about the importance of enduring failure in pursuit of success.

Now that you know about the Dunning-Kruger Effect, you'll start spotting it everywhere you go. You might be tempted to point out particular instances, especially in people you don't like. Draw on your willpower and resist the urge! Not only is it impossible to objectively prove that any one individual is suffering from the Dunning-Kruger Effect, but your analysis won't exactly make you popular even if you do happen to be right. The human ego is a fragile thing. We all like to think that we are special in some way, which is probably why most of us like to think we are somehow more skilled and logical than the average individual. Don't fall into the trap of thinking that just because you know the psychology behind it, you are in some way immune to this phenomenon. However successful you may become, don't forget that you are only human.

Finally, you can also use this theory to reassure yourself whenever you experience a period of self-doubt. It isn't fun to question your competence and pick over every little mistake or flaw, but at least it's a sign that you aren't overconfident. Ideally, you'll end up with a positive self-image and yet still question yourself from time to time. Remember that no-one is perfect, but that's actually one of the great things about life – without room to improve and grow, where would we be? Remain mindful, stay positive, bounce back from failure, and know that you can always push further. **May you enjoy your successes, learn from each experience, and always set yourself high standards!**

Good luck!

One last thing before you go – Can I ask you a favor? I need your help! If you like this book, **could you please share your experience on Amazon and write an honest review?** It will be just one minute for you (I will be happy even with one sentence!), **but a GREAT help for me and definitely a good Karma ☺.** Since I'm not a well-established author and I don't have powerful people and big publishing companies supporting me, <u>I read every single review and jump around with joy like a little kid every time my readers comment on my books and give me their honest feedback!</u> If I was able to inspire you in any way, please let me know! It will also help me get my books in front of more people looking for new ideas and useful knowledge.

http://tinyurl.com/reviewdiscipline

If you did not enjoy the book or had a problem with it, please don't hesitate to contact me at <u>contact@mindfulnessforsuccess.com</u> **and tell me how I can improve it to provide more value and more knowledge to my readers.** I'm constantly working on my books to make them better and more helpful.

Thank you and good luck! I believe in you and I wish you all the best on your new journey!
Your friend,
Ian

My Free Gift to You – <u>Get One of My Audiobooks For Free!</u>

If you've never created an account on Audible (the biggest audiobook store in the world), **you can claim one free audiobook of mine**!

It's a simple process:

1. Pick one of my audiobooks on Audible:

http://www.audible.com/search?advsearchKeywords=Ian+Tuhovsky

Shortened link: http://tinyurl.com/IanTuhovskyAudiobooks

2. Once you choose a book and open its detail page, click the orange button "Free with 30-Day Trial Membership."

3. Follow the instructions to create your account and download your first free audiobook.

Note that you are NOT obligated to continue after your free trial expires. You can cancel your free trial easily anytime, and you won't be charged at all.

Also, if you haven't downloaded your free book already:

Discover How to Get Rid of Stress & Anxiety and Reach Inner Peace in 20 Days or Less!

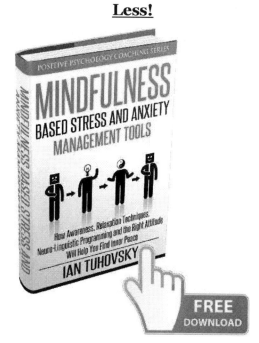

To help speed up your personal transformation, I have prepared a special gift for you!

Download my full, 120 page e-book "Mindfulness Based Stress and Anxiety Management Tools" for free by clicking here.

Link:

tinyurl.com/mindfulnessgift

Hey there like-minded friends, let's get connected!

Don't hesitate to visit:

-My Blog: www.mindfulnessforsuccess.com

-My Facebook fanpage: https://www.facebook.com/mindfulnessforsuccess

Recommended Reading for You:

If you are interested in Self-Development, NLP, Psychology, Social Dynamics, PR, Soft Skills and related topics, you might be interested in previewing or downloading my other books:

<u>Emotional Intelligence Training: A Practical Guide to Making Friends with Your Emotions and Raising Your EQ</u>

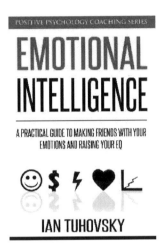

Do you believe your life would be healthier, happier and even better, if you had more practical strategies to regulate your own emotions? Most people agree with that.

Or, more importantly:

Do you believe you'd be healthier and happier if everyone who you live with had the strategies to regulate their emotions?

...Right?

The truth is not too many people actually realize what EQ is really all about and what causes its popularity to grow constantly.

Scientific research conducted by many American and European universities prove that the **"common" intelligence responses account for less than 20% of our life achievements and successes, while the other over 80% depends on emotional intelligence.** To put it roughly: **either you are emotionally intelligent, or you're doomed to mediocrity, at best.**

As opposed to the popular image, emotionally intelligent people are not the ones who react impulsively and spontaneously, or who act lively and fiery in all types of social environments.

Emotionally intelligent people are open to new experiences, can show feelings adequate to the situation, either good or bad, and find it easy to socialize with other people and establish new contacts. They handle stress well, say "no" easily, realistically assess the achievements of themselves or others and are not afraid of constructive criticism and taking calculated risks. **They are the people of success.** Unfortunately, this perfect model of an emotionally intelligent person is extremely rare in our modern times.

Sadly, nowadays, **the amount of emotional problems in the world is increasing at an alarming rate.** We are getting richer, but less and less happy. Depression, suicide, relationship breakdowns, loneliness of choice, fear of closeness, addictions—this is clear evidence that we are getting increasingly worse when it comes to dealing with our emotions.
Emotional intelligence is a SKILL, and can be learned through constant practice and training, just like riding a bike or swimming!

This book is stuffed with lots of effective exercises, helpful info and practical ideas. Every chapter covers different areas of emotional intelligence and shows you, **step by step**, what exactly you can do to **develop your EQ** and become the **better version of yourself**.
I will show you how freeing yourself from the domination of left-sided brain thinking can contribute to your inner transformation—**the emotional revolution that will help you redefine who you are and what you really want from life!**

In This Book I'll Show You:

• What Is Emotional Intelligence and What Does EQ Consist of?
• How to **Observe and Express** Your Emotions
• How to **Release Negative Emotions** and **Empower the Positive Ones**
• How to Deal with Your **Internal Dialogues**
• How to **Deal with the Past**
• **How to Forgive** Yourself and How to Forgive Others
• How to Free Yourself from **Other People's Opinions and Judgments**
• What Are "Submodalities" and How Exactly You Can Use Them to **Empower Yourself** and **Get Rid of Stress**
• The Nine Things You Need to **Stop Doing to Yourself**
• How to Examine Your Thoughts
• **Internal Conflicts** Troubleshooting Technique
• The Lost Art of Asking Yourself the Right Questions and **Discovering Your True Self!**
• How to Create Rich Visualizations
• LOTS of practical exercises from the mighty arsenal of psychology, family therapy, NLP etc.
• **And many, many more!**

Direct Buy Link to Amazon Kindle Store:
https://tinyurl.com/IanEQTrainingKindle
Paperback version on Createspace: https://tinyurl.com/ianEQpaperback

Communication Skills Training: A Practical Guide to Improving Your Social Intelligence, Presentation, Persuasion and Public Speaking

Do You Know How To Communicate With People Effectively, Avoid Conflicts and Get What You Want From Life?

...It's not only about what you say, but also about WHEN, WHY and HOW you say it.

Do The Things You Usually Say Help You, Or Maybe Hold You Back?

Have you ever considered **how many times you intuitively felt that maybe you lost something important or crucial, simply because you unwittingly said or did something, which put somebody off?** Maybe it was a misfortunate word, bad formulation, inappropriate joke, forgotten name, huge misinterpretation, awkward conversation or a strange tone of your voice?
Maybe you assumed that you knew exactly what a particular concept meant for another person and you stopped asking questions?
Maybe you could not listen carefully or could not stay silent for a moment? **How many times have you wanted to achieve something, negotiate better terms, or ask for a promotion and failed miserably?**

It's time to put that to an end with the help of this book.

Lack of communication skills is exactly what ruins most peoples' lives.
If you don't know how to communicate properly, you are going to have problems both in your intimate and family relationships.

You are going to be ineffective in work and business situations. It's going to be troublesome managing employees or getting what you want from your boss or your clients on a daily basis. Overall, **effective communication is like an engine oil which makes your life run**

smoothly, getting you wherever you want to be. There are very few areas in life in which you can succeed in the long run without this crucial skill.

What Will You Learn With This Book?

-What Are The **Most Common Communication Obstacles** Between People And How To Avoid Them

-How To Express Anger And Avoid Conflicts

-What Are **The Most 8 Important Questions You Should Ask Yourself** If You Want To Be An Effective Communicator?

-**5 Most Basic and Crucial** Conversational Fixes

-How To Deal With Difficult and Toxic People

-Phrases to **Purge from Your Dictionary** (And What to Substitute Them With)

-The Subtle Art of **Giving and Receiving Feedback**

-Rapport, the **Art of Excellent Communication**

-How to Use Metaphors to **Communicate Better** And **Connect With People**

-What Metaprograms and Meta Models Are and How Exactly To Make Use of Them To **Become A Polished Communicator**

-How To Read Faces and **How to Effectively Predict Future Behaviors**

-How to Finally Start **Remembering Names**

-How to Have a Great Public Presentation

-How To Create Your Own **Unique Personality** in Business (and Everyday Life)

-Effective Networking

Direct link to Amazon Kindle Store: https://tinyurl.com/IanCommSkillsKindle

Paperback version on Createspace:

http://tinyurl.com/iancommunicationpaperback

Confidence: Your Practical Training: How to Develop Healthy Self Esteem and Deep Self Confidence to Be Successful and Become True Friends with Yourself

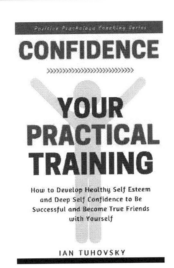

Have you ever considered how many opportunities you have missed and how many chances you have wasted by lacking self-confidence when you need it most? Have you ever given up on your plans, important goals, and dreams not because you just decided to focus on something else, but simply because you were too SCARED or hesitant to even start, or stick up to the plan and keep going?

Are you afraid of starting your own business or asking for a promotion? Petrified of public speaking, socializing, dating, taking up new hobbies, or going to job interviews?

Can you imagine how amazing and relieving it would feel to finally obtain all the self-esteem needed to accomplish things you've always wanted to achieve in your life?

Finally, have you ever found yourself in a situation where you simply couldn't understand **WHY you acted in a certain way**, or why you kept holding yourself back and feeling all the bad emotions, instead of just going for what's the most important to you?

Due to early social conditioning and many other influences, most people on this planet are already familiar with all these feelings.

WAY TOO FAMILIAR!

I know how it feels, too. I was in the same exact place.

And then, I found the way!

It's high time you did something about it too because, truth be told, self-confident people just have it way easier in every single aspect of life!

From becoming your own boss or succeeding in your career, through dating and socializing, to starting new hobbies, standing up for yourself or maybe finally packing your suitcase and going on this Asia trip you promised yourself decades ago... All too often, people fail in these quests as they aren't equipped with the natural and lasting self-confidence to deal with them in a proper way.

Confidence is not useful only in everyday life and casual situations. Do you really want to fulfill your wildest dreams, or do you just want to keep chatting about them with your friends, until one day you wake up as a grumpy, old, frustrated person?
Big achievements require brave and fearless actions. If you want to act bravely, you need to be confident.

Along with lots of useful, practical exercises, this book will provide you with plenty of new information that will help you understand what confidence problems really come down to. And this is the most important and the saddest part, because most people do not truly recognize the root problem, and that's why they get poor results.

Lack of self-confidence and problems with unhealthy self-esteem are usually the reason why smart, competent, and talented people never achieve a satisfying life; a life that should easily be possible for them.

In this book, you will read about:
-How, when, and why society robs us all of natural confidence and healthy self-esteem.
-What kind of social and psychological traps you need to avoid in order to feel much calmer, happier, and more confident.
-What "natural confidence" means and how it becomes natural.
-What "self-confidence" really is and what it definitely isn't (as opposed to what most people think!).
-How your mind hurts you when it really just wants to help you, and how to stop the process.
-What different kinds of fear we feel, where they come from, and how to defeat them.
-How to have a great relationship with yourself.
-How to use stress to boost your inner strength.
-Effective and ineffective ways of building healthy self-esteem.
-Why the relation between self-acceptance and stress is so crucial.
-How to stay confident in professional situations.
-How to protect your self-esteem when life brings you down, and how to deal with criticism and jealousy.
-How to use neuro-linguistic programming, imagination, visualizations, diary entries, and your five senses to re-program your subconscious and get rid of "mental viruses" and detrimental beliefs that actively destroy your natural confidence and healthy self-esteem.
Take the right action and start changing your life for the better today!

Meditation for Beginners: How to Meditate (as an Ordinary Person!) to Relieve Stress and Be Successful

Meditation doesn't have to be about crystals, hypnotic folk music and incense sticks! **Forget about sitting in unnatural and uncomfortable positions while going, "Ommmmm...."** It is not necessarily a club full of yoga masters, Shaolin monks, hippies and new-agers.

It is a super useful and universal practice which can improve your overall brain performance and happiness. When meditating, you take a step back from actively thinking your thoughts, and instead see them for what they are. The reason why meditation is helpful in reducing stress and attaining peace is that it gives your over-active consciousness a break.

Just like your body needs it, your mind does too!

I give you the gift of peace that I was able to attain through present moment awareness.

Zen: Beginner's Guide: Happy, Peaceful and Focused Lifestyle for Everyone

Contrary to popular belief, Zen is not a discipline reserved for monks practicing Kung Fu. Although there is some truth to this idea, Zen is a practice that is applicable, useful and pragmatic for anyone to study regardless of what religion you follow (or don't follow).

Zen is the practice of studying your subconscious and **seeing your true nature.** The purpose of this work is to show you how to apply and utilize the teachings and essence of Zen in everyday life in the Western society. I'm not really an "absolute truth seeker" unworldly type of person—I just believe in practical plans and blueprints that actually help in living a better life. Of course I will tell you about the origin of Zen and the traditional ways of practicing it, but I will also show you my side of things, my personal point of view and translation of many Zen truths into a more "contemporary" and practical language.
It is a "modern Zen lifestyle" type of book.

What You Will Read About:
• Where Did Zen Come from? - A short history and explanation of Zen
• What Does Zen Teach? - The major teachings and precepts of Zen
• Various Zen meditation techniques that are applicable and practical for everyone!
• The Benefits of a Zen Lifestyle
• What Zen Buddhism is NOT?
• How to Slow Down and Start Enjoying Your Life
• How to Accept Everything and Lose Nothing
• Why Being Alone Can Be Beneficial
• Why Pleasure Is NOT Happiness
• Six Ways to Practically Let Go
• How to De-clutter Your Life and Live Simply
• "Mindfulness on Steroids"
• How to Take Care of Your Awareness and Focus
• Where to Start and How to Practice Zen as a Regular Person
• And many other interesting concepts...

I invite you to take this journey into the peaceful world of Zen Buddhism with me today!
Direct Buy Link to Amazon Kindle Store: https://tinyurl.com/IanZenGuide

Buddhism: Beginner's Guide: Bring Peace and Happiness to Your Everyday Life

Buddhism is one of the most practical and simple belief systems on this planet, and it has greatly helped me on my way to become a better person in every aspect possible. In this book I will show you what happened and how it was.

No matter if you are totally green when it comes to Buddha's teachings or maybe you have already heard something about them—this book will help you systematize your knowledge and will inspire you to learn more and to take steps to make your life positively better!

I invite you to take this beautiful journey into the graceful and meaningful world of Buddhism with me today!

Direct link to Amazon Kindle Store: https://tinyurl.com/IanBuddhismGuide
Paperback version on Createspace: http://tinyurl.com/ianbuddhismpaperback

About The Author

Author's Blog: www.mindfulnessforsuccess.com

Amazon Author Page: http://www.amazon.com/author/iantuhovsky/

Instagram profile: https://instagram.com/mindfulnessforsuccess

Hi! I'm Ian...

. . . and I am interested in life. I am in the study of having an awesome and passionate life, which I believe is within the reach of practically everyone. I'm not a mentor or a guru. I'm just a guy who always knew there was more than we are told. I managed to turn my life around from way below my expectations to a really satisfying one, and now I want to share this fascinating journey with you so that you can do it, too.

I was born and raised somewhere in Eastern Europe, where Polar Bears eat people on the streets, we munch on snow instead of ice cream and there's only vodka instead of tap water, but since I make a living out of several different businesses, I move to a new country every couple of months. I also work as an HR consultant for various European companies.

I love self-development, traveling, recording music and providing value by helping others. I passionately read and write about social psychology, sociology, NLP, meditation, mindfulness, eastern philosophy, emotional intelligence, time management, communication skills and all of the topics related to conscious self-development and being the most awesome version of yourself.

Breathe. Relax. Feel that you're alive and smile. And never hesitate to contact me!

Made in the USA
San Bernardino, CA
19 August 2017